THE POWER
PARTNERSHIP

A Life of Miracles for Every Believer

Jonathan Conrathe
with Ralph Turner

malcolm down

PUBLISHING

Commendations

In church life today, much attention is quite rightly being given to strategy, missional thinking and goal-setting. However, without the power and presence of the Holy Spirit, these things can become techniques or management skills. Jonathan, in this book, brings us back to our radical foundations. We desperately need to see the gospel shared in word, works and in demonstration of God's power. The emerging generation needs to encounter God and should not jettison the gifts of the Holy Spirit. This book will prove to be a highly valuable resource. Our world is waiting for good news that has the power to transform lives and communities; it is waiting for the message of hope.

Stuart Bell
Leader of the Ground Level network and senior pastor of Alive Church

Jonathan was called to the Christian ministry at the age of seventeen. He started out as a full-time evangelist two years later. Now, thirty years on, this book lets us in on Jonathan's story and his passion for every one of us to experience the power of the Holy Spirit equipping us to see our world changed. Reading this book will be both an encouragement and a challenge.

Steve Clifford
General director, Evangelical Alliance

Jonathan Conrathe is an inspiration – he has travelled the world seeing salvations, healings and restorations. Here he tells his amazing stories, unpacks scriptures and the result, I pray, is that in it all we will not leave it to the professionals, but as Jonathan explains – this is for the whole Church. Thank you, Jonathan, for consistency, faith and making room for God to do what we cannot.

Gerald Coates
Founder of Pioneer network, speaker, author, broadcaster

Inspiring, brave, humorous and powerful in God's grace – that's my friend Jon Conrathe; and *The Power Partnership* pulsates with the same grace that is on his life. This book will place a theological foundation beneath your feet, it will stir you to action, teach you the steps of how to flow with the Holy Spirit, and align you in the very purposes of the kingdom's power. I think we will be using this outstanding book among our congregations and in our training academy for years to come. Thank you, Jon and Ralph!

Jarrod Cooper
Senior leader, Revive Church

The gospel of the kingdom is a power gospel with all the gifts of the Holy Spirit demonstrating that power. Jonathan has preached the power gospel in many nations of the world for many years and has seen thousands receive salvation. This is an excellent book which covers all the gifts and contains solid teaching for those who want more of the reality of God's power.

Don Double
Founder and evangelist, Good News Crusade

The three things that impressed me as I read were freshness, faith and foundations. This book is fresh with living relationship with God; it puts active faith at the heart of everything in the Christian life, and it presents baptism in the Holy Spirit and spiritual gifts as foundational to ministry.

These three values are particularly relevant today. While applauding the emergence of charismatic and Pentecostal scholars who can engage in academic theological circles and seminar with distinction, it must be said that knowing about our Lord is not the same as knowing Him.

Jonathan breathes faith through his writing, a faith that is active and does things, not least in healing and deliverance. His repeated phrase is 'stepping out' in faith. Five hundred years after Luther reminded the European Church that it was justified by faith, we still need to define faith, as James' epistle does, as that which works! Not just doing our own works but rather giving God the opportunity to do His works through us.

This book is a challenge to all Christians, especially leaders. It is so easy to abandon our first love and our first faith and settle for the safety and security of the institutional structures of church life. We need a fresh stepping out of believers who are baptised in the Holy Spirit, moving in spiritual gifts, and reaching the nation and nations with the life and power of the gospel.

Thank you, Jonathan for keeping this challenge before us in your book – may it bear much fruit!

Roger T. Forster
Ichthus Christian Fellowship

Packed full of biblical principles and relevant stories, *The Power Partnership* is a rallying call to partner with the Holy Spirit.

Jonathan's passion and excitement for the gospel is contagious. This book has inspired me afresh to step out of my comfort zone expectantly.

Andy Frost
Director, Share Jesus International

Jesus did not give His life just so we could be saved and go to heaven one day. He gave it so that the presence and power of His Spirit would be restored to humankind, in order to effect the entire world with the works of His kingdom. Using step by step, vividly clear teaching, illustrations and testimonies, Jonathan's new book encourages, informs and inspires all of us to rise up in faith, expecting a constant flow of miracles and to live the life Jesus died for us to live. I highly recommend you read it.

Wynne Goss
Co-founder, inHOPE Ministries

Both Ralph and Jonathan carry a passion for people and for missions. Their desire to see people radically connected to Jesus and building strong relationships that influence their communities is infectious. Whenever you talk with them they will first challenge you to reach out and then embolden you to do it. So go on a journey and discover how you can bring change in your world.

Rachel Hickson
Founding director, Heartcry for Change

This really is an exciting book. It deals with the baptism of the Spirit and the spiritual gifts in a practical and inspiring way. The teaching throughout is clear, and the stories of how the gifts of the

6

Spirit have been used in Jonathan's evangelistic ministry could not be more thrilling. However, this is more than a manual laced with relevant and eye-opening illustrations; it is a call to action and an appeal to us all to enter into an increasingly powerful personal partnership with God the Holy Spirit. Read the book and rise to the challenge!

Hugh Osgood
President of Churches in Communities International and co-chair of the UK Charismatic and Pentecostal Leaders' Conference

Jon has a passion for souls; his message is pure and heartfelt. He shares the gospel boldly and with confidence and helps ignite a fire in many hearts – mine included! In Jonathan's new book he shares compelling stories. We learn about partnering with God and believing that God can do amazing things through ordinary people who trust in an extraordinary God. As you read this book, expect God to do miracles for you and through you. God is inviting you into a partnership with Him.

Chris Overstreet
Outreach pastor, Bethel Church and Bethel School of Supernatural Ministry, Redding, California

This book represents the passionate outpouring of Jonathan's heart and expresses the very core of his life's message – living in a power partnership with the Holy Spirit! His retelling of biblical stories and his many personal accounts of partnering with the Holy Spirit are both faith-building and inspirational. Power partnership with the Holy Spirit was the foundation for Jesus' amazing ministry on earth – as it was also for Jesus' disciples. This offer of partnership has never been withdrawn and Jonathan explains how we, as Jesus' current disciples on earth, may access this for ourselves in the here and now. This is a book to read and then do – and to keep rereading and re-doing!

Ian Rossol
All Nations Church, Leicester

Jonathan Conrathe has vast experience of seeing God's supernatural power working through his life. In step-by-step teaching, Jonathan shows that this privilege is for every believer. Whether you are a new Christian or someone who has been in church leadership for decades, *The Power Partnership* is a resource for you.

Ashley Schmierer
International president of INC Churches

As a healing evangelist, Jonathan's life is characterised by a radical openness to the person and work of the Holy Spirit and a passion to see multitudes come to Christ. *The Power Partnership* is written to encourage all believers to be filled with the Spirit, to exercise the gifts of the Spirit and to grow in Spirit-empowered evangelism. Read and be inspired!

Dave Smith
Senior pastor, KingsGate Community Church

I have been saying for a while that we must contend for New Testament theology, New Testament power and New Testament lifestyle. Jonathan's new book is an answer to that contending cry of the Holy Spirit. The message is timely and carries a prophetic call to every believer to walk in the fullness of New Testament power available through the cross of Christ and the empowering of the Holy Spirit. Jonathan encouragingly teaches from personal experience as a practitioner and yet roots the message in the orthodoxy of Scripture. This book has the potential to set every reader on fire!

Steve Uppal
Senior leader, All Nations Christian Centre, Wolverhampton

First published 2017 by Malcolm Down Publishing Ltd.
www.malcolmdown.co.uk

British Library Cataloguing in Publication Data
A catalogue record for this book is available from the British Library.

ISBN 978-1-910786-76-5

Cover design by Esther Kotecha
Art direction by Sarah Grace

Printed in the UK by Bell and Bain Ltd, Glasgow

Dedication

I unreservedly dedicate this book to the Lord Jesus Christ, my Saviour and Redeemer, the One to whom every knee shall bow and every tongue confess He is Lord! You are 'the desire of all nations' (Haggai 2:7, KJV), worthy of our every breath, and highest praise.

Jonathan Conrathe

Thank you from Jon:

There are always so many people in our lives who deserve not only a mention but a much greater thank you than an entry in a book such as this can provide. I must limit myself to a few who have had, and continue to have a profound impact on my life and ministry. First and foremost, to my sweetheart, wife and very best friend, Elaine. Your love, encouragement and patience has helped and strengthened me more than the world will ever know. You have been, and continue to be God's great gift to myself and our boys. Thank you. I love you and am honoured to be your husband.

To our three sons, Nathan, Joshua and Benjamin. Time and again you have selflessly given your father to the many we have been called to reach for Christ. Heaven applauds you! Our times together are precious and carried in my heart. Each one of you are uniquely gifted and called by God and you will all grow to be great men in His kingdom. You are always loved, by God, and by Mum and myself. I am honoured to be your dad.

Thanks are also due to my parents, Michael and Jill Conrathe, who first taught me to love the Word of God and the ministry of the Holy Spirit. You have set a great example, and have loved and believed in me every step of the way. Thank you. Mum and Dad, you're the best!

To Sheena Pailthorpe, and her late husband, David. You taught me to listen to the voice of God, and to be a worshipper. You and your family have stood by me, and walked with me through some of life's toughest challenges. I will always be grateful.

Much gratitude also to Don Double, one of God's great evangelists. Thank you for believing in me as a young nineteen-year-old, and giving your time and energy to train me in the ministry God called me to. You told me in the first week that I travelled with you that you always pray for every evangelist you train to accomplish more than you did – but that you would give me a run for my money! I am still trying to catch up! Your faith, integrity, passion for Jesus and love for the lost have forever marked my life.

Last, but by no means least, big thanks are due to my friend and colleague, Ralph Turner, who took up the challenge of turning the transcripts of my messages on the Holy Spirit into a faith-building, readable book. Although we have both done a fair bit of writing, it was Ralph who did all the foundational work of putting the spoken word into readable form. You've done a great job, Ralph! Thank you.

Thank you from Ralph:

My love and thanks as always to Roh, my amazing wife. Love to the broader Turner family; four children and two grandchildren (Hi, Jessica and Abigail!). Thank you to my wonderful proof reader, Ali Pereira, who has done a great job as always. And thanks to Malcolm Down and Sarah Griggs for your continued faith in me.

A note on reading this book

We have deliberately included many Bible references in the footnotes. They are there to enable you to study each subject in greater depth. We encourage you to do so.

We have also included an appendix which offers further study on each chapter. This will be useful for personal study, and particularly for home groups and discussion groups.

Books by Jonathan Conrathe

Radical Christianity

Books by Ralph Turner

Working for God
The God-Life
Cheating Death, Living Life: Linda's Story
Gerald Coates: Pioneer

Contents

Contents

Introduction

I knew something had changed the moment they came in the door. Mum and Dad were back from a weekend away. As I came down the stairs to greet them, they looked different. It was as if there was a light around them that emanated from a sense of power. They were smiling – almost laughing as they greeted me. As a nine-year-old boy, I could feel a strong presence there in that hallway. Even then, although I wasn't sure what it was they had, I could feel the purity and power of it and a hunger to know more was birthed in my heart.

Mum had been baptised in the Spirit for some time. But for Dad, this was very much a step-by-step process. They had been visiting Ian and Rosemary Andrews in Chard, Somerset, in the south-west of England. God was doing some amazing things at the Chard Christian Fellowship, and both my parents were powerfully impacted by it. Dad had been struggling somewhat with what it meant to have a real experience of the baptism in the Holy Spirit. But that weekend, having been prayed for and challenged by Rosemary to step out in faith where speaking in tongues was concerned, Dad began to give voice to the growing thirst in his heart, and started to speak a few words in a language he had neither learned or spoken in before. That night, at the evening service in Chard, he was well and truly filled with the Holy Spirit. So much so, he was utterly overwhelmed with the Presence of God and continued worshipping and speaking in other tongues for several hours, even as the rest of the meeting went on around him!

Dad changed that day. A new grace and gentleness came into his life. He was still the strong father I had known him to be, but from that point forward he became a gentle giant; approachable, loving and wise – and operating in a genuine partnership with the Holy Spirit, in his preaching, prayer life and ministry in the gifts of the Spirit.

I couldn't have ignored it even if I had wanted to. For us, it meant a change of church and a new beginning in what became known as the Cheam Fellowship. My own hunger for whatever God had for me began to grow and I wanted to experience for myself what Mum and Dad were evidently already walking in.

As a young boy, I became profoundly aware of the presence and power of the Holy Spirit, especially in church meetings. I would often observe how God was moving. I would see when the Spirit was upon someone in a powerful way.

It was not long until that same baptism in the Spirit was my own personal experience. And in receiving the Holy Spirit, in being baptised in the Holy Spirit, it has changed my life. From that point on, I began to experience increasing manifestations of His presence, gifts and power, coupled with an increasing hunger to share the good news of Jesus with those who didn't yet know Him.

I wanted to be sure that what I had was real and I was excited to see what had happened to me was so clearly in God's Word, the Bible. This outpouring of God's Spirit drew me in even more to the Word of God. I couldn't stop reading, hungry to learn more of this power of the Holy Spirit, as demonstrated in the lives and ministry of Jesus and His apostles.

Years have passed. Mum and Dad have remained as radical as ever and, knowing this was never intended to be a one-off experience, I continue to press in for more of Him too, believing that everything is available in Christ.

Having had a vision of Jesus calling me to Christian ministry at the age of seventeen, I started out as a full-time evangelist two years later, aged nineteen, under the care and mentoring of Don Double. These last nearly thirty years have been a time of challenge and blessing. Mission24 has been the vehicle for me to preach the gospel around the world in nearly fifty countries. And always with 'signs following' (Mark 16:20, KJV). Hundreds of thousands have come to Christ; new churches have been planted in unreached areas. There has been healing, deliverance and even some resurrections from the dead. None of this would have been possible without having met God through His Holy Spirit in such a powerful way. None of it possible without that power partnership.

And that's the message of this book. I want to invite you on a journey as we discover the ways of the Holy Spirit, as we begin to enjoy and appreciate a power partnership with Him; a life of miracles for every believer. Learn with me as we find how we can move in that very same anointing in our daily lives. As believers in Christ we can learn to cooperate with the Holy Spirit in the supernatural gifts that God gives us. Let's learn together how we can experience the love of the Father, the power of the cross, and the anointing of the Spirit every day of our lives. This power partnership is for you, for me… and for the thousands of lives that are going to be changed because we are willing to live and minister God's way.

Jonathan Conrathe
Bourne, Lincolnshire
2017

Chapter One:
The Authority of the Believer

The purpose of this book is simple. God can change the world, and can do so through you and me. When the final page of the book is turned, with God's help, we will be further equipped and able to help that change.

Paul teaches in his letter to the Church in Rome[1] that we have the same power in us that raised Jesus from the dead.

For some of us, that may be just a verse we quote, but as Spirit-filled Christians we really *do* have that power. We have an authority as believers that, when we exercise it, means that anything and everything around us changes.

Strengthened faith

For that verse to be true in our experience, we need to start from a position of faith. We need to believe the promises of the Bible! This book will take us through many of those promises. We'll consider them and apply them. It's all there – in God's Word. Paul speaks pretty strongly on the whole subject and particularly with regard to walking in the ways of the Holy Spirit. He says to the Galatians in no uncertain terms:

> You foolish Galatians! Who has bewitched you? Before your very eyes Jesus Christ was clearly portrayed as crucified. I would like to learn just one thing from you: did you receive the Spirit by the works of the law, or by believing what you heard? Are you so foolish? After beginning by means of the Spirit, are you now trying to finish by means of the flesh?[2]

And there it is. There's our dilemma. So many start well in these things. Then, because of the world we live in, because we have been taught from a young age to only believe what we see with our own eyes, many of us start to make excuses for lack of power, sometimes deciding it's all to do with rules and regulations. What we do, how we do it. So even when we do reach out and pray for someone, we follow an in-built rule book in our minds on what to do and what not to do. It's easy to forget that we are partnering with the Holy Spirit. It is He who can speak to us as to how to pray and minister. It is He who heals; it is through the Holy Spirit that we see miracles, and we must learn again to depend on Him.

The passage in Galatians is so empowering! It teaches us that the Spirit is not given because of our performance but entirely because of Christ's sacrifice. It's to do with our faith in His finished work,[3] His gracious *gift* of righteousness, and *gift* of the Holy Spirit, rather than our own efforts! That means that we don't have to be experts. We don't have to have been Christians for a certain number of years. He has given every one of us full access to the power of the Holy Spirit. Every one of us can enjoy a power partnership with Him.

So, strengthen your faith! Let's make sure that we are reading the Word of God, believing what it says and listening to the Holy Spirit. Some of us concentrate on the Word of God, the Bible, for our inspiration. Others of us speak of listening to the Spirit. But it's not 'either/or'. It's both the Word *and* the Spirit. Let's be a 'both/and' people. Someone once said that if all you have is the Word, you'll dry up, if all you have is the Spirit, you'll blow up, but if you have both the Word and the Spirit, you'll grow up. As we study this book together, let God begin to encourage you. Unlike our physical body, we can continue to grow spiritually, whatever our age. Are you ready to grow?

Lambs among wolves

When Jesus sent out the disciples to heal and to declare God's kingdom, they went as simple believers. He instructed them to take nothing with them. They had no money, no supplies; nothing other than themselves, the anointing of the Holy Spirit, and their faith. But that faith was in the power and authority of Christ![4] They went as 'lambs among wolves',[5] but that faith was sufficient. Operating in the power and authority Christ gave them, they returned to Him with amazing stories of the enemy defeated. Jesus said:

> I saw Satan fall like lightning from heaven. Behold, I have given you authority to tread on serpents and scorpions, and over all the power of the enemy, and nothing shall hurt you.[6]

There it is. The authority of the believer. We may feel we are vulnerable – that's the picture Scripture paints. Lambs are easy prey. But even in the presence of wolves, we are protected. Wolves can't harm us. Serpents and scorpions can't touch us. Simple believers we may be – but simple believers with the power and authority of Christ. The issue is not us as lambs. The issue is who is with us; who we represent, and who is protecting us. As He sends us out, so He is with us in all we do, backing us up with His authority and power.

In fact, later on in the same passage, Jesus describes the disciples as 'babes' or 'little children'.[7] Again it's a picture of us as defenceless. Babes we may be. But guess who our protective Father is!

Jesus speaks of giving us authority. The word 'authority' in Greek is *exousia*. It means the right to act. It is a delegated authority. Jesus will back us up in His power as we go out in His name. He gives us the right to act! Just as Jesus sent out the disciples, so He sends us. We have the same power and authority. He is with us in exactly the same way.

I was once in Uganda and came to a border post. There in front of me stood a nine-year-old boy with a rifle in his hands. He asked for my passport. What did I do? Did I say, 'No, you're only a child, I'm not going to listen to you!'? No, of course not! He had a rifle in his hands. I was very quick to comply with his request! It's not that we are lambs or babes that is the issue. It's that in His name we have the authority of Christ, the *exousia*, the right to act in His power, in our very hands!

We may feel like we are beginners. We may feel like babes or little children. We may make the mistakes any little child may make – we may trip over ourselves, we may not have the words to say. But the Bible says it is enough. We have, as little children, overcome the world[8] because of who is in us and the authority we carry in Him.

When we are baptised in the Spirit, we have an active power partnership and we are able to operate in the authority Christ gives us. And like the early disciples, we will see great things accomplished – a life of miracles for every believer.

The key to operating in the authority of Jesus is submission to Him, believing and obeying – stepping out in faith in His Word. The key to ministering in His power is baptism in the Holy Spirit. This is the doorway to the power partnership we are called to.

Have you received the Holy Spirit?

There is a commonly held view among some Christians. It's this: 'When I was born again, I got everything. I was filled with the Holy Spirit at that point. I don't need anything more.' But that's simply not in line with Scripture. It may be true in principle, but it certainly needs to be received and walked out in experience. The famous preacher Dr Martyn Lloyd-Jones once said:

We say, 'Ah well, I am already baptised with the Spirit; it happened when I was born again, at my conversion; there is nothing for me to seek, I have got it all'. Got it all? Well, if you have got it all, I simply ask in the name of God, why are you as you are?[9]

If it's really true that we get it all at conversion, in the name of God why are so many believers living powerless, spiritually impotent lives? The famous old preacher doesn't mince his words. And nor will this book. There may be people reading this who have resisted the whole idea of being baptised in the Holy Spirit. Often it's because of what we have been taught in our particular background or denomination. But if we really want to have God's best in our life, if we want that 'same power'[10] in our life that Paul talks about, if we want to operate in Christ's authority and in power partnership with the Holy Spirit, there is a need to change our theological views!

Kids' camp

You read my parents' story in the introduction. It's my story too. Following on from my early observations of the changes in Mum and Dad, I first powerfully encountered the Holy Spirit at the age of nine on a kids' camp near Chard. The very same place Dad had his own experience of the Holy Spirit. I'm not from a Pentecostal background, and I'd never heard much as to who the Holy Spirit was until that point of encountering Him. But as a nine-year- old child, suddenly, I knew how real He was.

God flooded my very being, and I was overwhelmed, sensing His presence. I felt such a Holy Spirit anointing on me. It was the start of a lifetime of an awareness of the Holy Spirit in my life; the start of a lifetime of learning the ways of the Holy Spirit. Many experience a full release of the gift of tongues when they are baptised in the Spirit, but for me that came a bit later after I realised that I had to do the speaking, trusting the Holy Spirit to give me the words. But once I started speaking in tongues, building my faith through the Word and learning to praise and worship the Lord with greater freedom, I started to hear the gentle whisperings of the Spirit and grew in expectation for the Holy Spirit to move. I grew in expectation that when I prayed for people, I would experience the joy of seeing God move in power time and again. Knowing Him more made me long for Him more. And growing up in a church where the people were given the freedom to minister in the gifts of the Spirit during the services was a great training ground in learning to recognise when the Holy Spirit was manifestly moving and when He appeared not to be.

One of the truths of life in God's kingdom, as expressed by Jesus, is that we have to come as children to the Father. To enter His kingdom, to operate in His power, we need to be as children.[11] In a way, we all need to go back to kids' camp, to set aside our poor experiences, our assumptions and our lack of faith in the past, and believe what the Word of God says.

Being baptised in the Holy Spirit

Maybe, as you have started reading this book, you have a growing desire to be baptised in the Holy Spirit yourself? In Jesus' teaching on the Holy Spirit found in John's Gospel,[12] Jesus promised to send us 'another Helper'[13]. In Greek, the word 'another' means someone who is just the same as Jesus, but different in that He doesn't have a physical body like Jesus. Essentially, Jesus was saying that the Holy Spirit will do for us, in us, and through us the same things Jesus would have done were He with us in the flesh as He was while He ministered on the earth 2,000 years ago! When I consider the ministry of Jesus, that's an exciting proposition. The Holy Spirit is 'the promise of the Father'[14] and although the world cannot receive Him, if you are a child of God through faith in Jesus, you can simply come to Father God and ask Him to fill you with His Holy Spirit. Luke's Gospel assures us that we will receive exactly what we ask for.[15] I would encourage you, if you have already given your life to Jesus, to take a few moments right now, to stop, and come to God in prayer, asking Him to baptise you with the Holy Spirit. Maybe you would like to use the prayer below to help you:

Heavenly Father, I thank You for Your gift of love, Jesus Christ, who took all my sins, died and rose to life that I might be saved. I want to tell the world about Him. I need Your Holy Spirit. I am thirsty for His power. I want to live for You and win others to You. Please fill me now with the Holy Spirit, release me in Your gifts, and give me the ability to speak in tongues that I might stay full of Your life and power to glorify Your name and reach other people with the good news of Your Son. Holy Spirit, I receive You now, in Jesus' name.

Now go ahead and receive His power, His fullness... lift your hands and thank Him by faith, worshipping Him, and start to speak out in a new language as God gives you the ability. It's a step of faith... start speaking and the Lord will release rivers of 'living water'[16] within you.

For those of you already baptised in the Holy Spirit, why not take time now to refresh yourself in Him? Begin to speak out in tongues and invite God to fill you afresh.

Creating a thirst for the things of God

As you read these words, allow God to create a thirst in you. When you are really thirsty, you *have* to have a drink. I remember as a boy, setting out on a walk. It was in the holidays and I was totally unprepared. By the time I got to a cold water tap, I was desperately dehydrated. I drank a pint of water straight off!

How dehydrated are you? Are you just drinking enough to get by? Or are you really thirsty for the things of God? Are you content with where you are, or do you want *all* the Holy Spirit has for you? Maybe you have just prayed that prayer in the last section and asked God to fill you with his Holy Spirit. If so, that's just the start. Stay thirsty for more. Don't ever get content with a small trickle of water. Get so thirsty you drink a pint of water straight off! Get so thirsty, you want to dive in, to soak yourself in all God has for you.

I remember ministering in a FGBMFI (Full Gospel Businessmen's Fellowship International) meeting in Surrey, England, where a young boy, who had come with his dad, came up to me and said, 'I'm so desperate for the Holy Spirit, and I really want to speak in tongues… will you pray for me?' I responded positively, and explained to him that I would lay hands on him and Jesus would fill him with the Holy Spirit, and give him power, and a new heavenly language to help him steward the power he would receive. I rested my hand on him, and before I could get any words out of my mouth in prayer, he gushed out in other tongues, like an unstoppable force! I was amazed how God just responded to his simple faith and thirst for the Holy Spirit – he just believed what I'd said, that when I laid my hands on him he'd be filled with the Spirit, and God met him there. What a contrast to those who come reluctantly, feeling as if they have to because they've finally lost a long verse by verse theological debate with God about the necessity of being baptised in the Holy Spirit! I often observe these kinds of people rarely receive much manifest power. So often our experience is dictated by our thirst. Come to Jesus in simple faith; keep coming, keep believing, and keep drinking of the life-giving Spirit of God, and the rivers will keep flowing!

An exchanged life

God wants every New Testament believer to move in the power of the Holy Spirit, to know what it is to live in the power of the Spirit.[17] Every Christian should be walking in the authority they have as a believer. It's very hard to live the Christian life without the power of the Spirit of God. If we try, we fail. The New Testament describes the Christian life as walking in the Spirit, keeping in step with the Spirit. It's simply not possible to live the Christian life without the help of the Holy Spirit. This is a power partnership and He, the Spirit, is the senior partner. He comes alongside us in partnership. The Greek word used in the Bible[18] when Jesus described the Holy Spirit as the 'Helper' is *parakletos*. It means 'one who comes alongside to help'.

I remember a good number of years ago in the early days of my ministry when, on the last night of a week-long mission, when I was exhausted and wanting to go home, everyone who had previously not responded for prayer during the last six days suddenly decided to respond at the last meeting. I felt so empty, but out of a sense of duty began to quickly lay hands on people and pray for them to be healed. Nothing was happening, and I was getting increasingly frustrated. After about ten minutes I stopped, convicted that I was not serving the people as well as I should. I turned to the Lord in prayer and told Him of my emptiness, confessed my frustration and asked Him to come and fill me again with His love and power to meet the needs of the people. Suddenly, as I stopped striving and rested back into Him, trusting Him to flow out of me in grace, I felt a fresh release of power go through me, coupled with great compassion. Many were healed and set free that night, and I returned home refreshed by the ministry of the Holy Spirit. Let us learn to depend on Him, and drink deeply of His supply. He is a constant source of life, energy and power.

The Bible also says if you walk in the Spirit, you will not fulfil the lusts of the flesh.[19] We all face the temptations and trials of life, but rather than focusing on the battle, there is a higher way to live, a greater flow of life that we can walk in which helps us overcome. We need to know what it is to live in the Spirit. It's living a higher life. An exchanged life. We allow God to exchange our imperfect, half-life for God's full life. There is a God-life for us to enjoy. When we ask God to change our life and when we are baptised in the Holy Spirit, learning to stay full of His life and following His promptings and leadings, we have that power of God in operation. Power to live. Power to overcome. And power to witness.[20]

With that power comes an ability not just to live better, but to minister to others as well. God wants every Christian to know what it is to minister in the power of God. No exceptions. It's not just for leaders; it's for every one of us.

Our old life is exchanged for a new life in Christ. The price paid was a high one. God's own Son died so we can have that exchanged life. A powerful life of living God's way and being able to speak that life out, to minister to others, to see other lives changed.

Let's not live with that new life only partly revealed in us. Let's go for the whole thing. Go on; jump into the river of God. Soak yourself. Following Jesus' directions, keep coming, keep drinking, keep believing. And the rivers of God will keep flowing.[21] His promise is sure!

The need
Based on current population numbers, if every Christian in the

world today led just four people to Christ, the whole world would be saved overnight. But we've had a problem. Our problem has been that only 10 per cent of the Church has been doing 100 per cent of the work.

God is changing the statistics. Pentecostal and charismatic churches are growing faster than any denominational church on the face of the planet. And there's a reason for that. It's not to do with denominations. It's all to do with Jesus saying 'you shall receive power when the Holy Spirit has come upon you; and you shall be witnesses to Me.'[22] And it's to do with people believing that scripture! Do you want to be part of the fastest growing section of the Church in the world today? Do you want to help further change the statistics? If so, be an authentic witness to Jesus Christ; be full of the power of the Spirit. It's a power partnership.

I have been privileged to preach the gospel in forty-seven nations – and counting. I have preached to almost every different religious group in the world. And I can tell you that when you stand on a platform before thousands of Muslims or Hindus, for example, and you present to them that Jesus is the Son of God, they kind of look at you and, well… they don't believe you. They've got their so-called Holy Book and they want an argument about that. So what are you going to do? You've got a black leather-bound book with gilt-edged pages and you say, 'Look, here it is – I'll prove that Jesus is the Son of God.' And they get out another book called the Koran or the Vedas, and they are looking forward to having an argument with you. It really doesn't get any of us very far.

The way to see people come from other religions to Christ is to minister to them in the power of God. They get healed. They see miracles. They receive visions and dreams. They see and feel His love in us, and get a sense of the Holy Spirit at work. They realise who the real God is.

Not so long ago it was reported that Muslim leaders in Africa expressed concern that they were losing ground daily to Christians because the Christian believers were healing the sick and raising the dead. Our brothers and sisters in Africa believe the Word, and their faith leads them to action that releases the power of the Spirit. They act on the Word. This is normal New Testament Christianity.

God works through His Holy Spirit in other ways too. He works sovereignly, especially when Christians are not around or not able to share the good news. Jesus appears to people in visions, dreams and revelations. Luke records this as a particular work of the Spirit in these last days.[23] And when that happens, Muslims and people of other faiths turn to the Lord in large numbers.

The Spirit speaks

There's a particular passage in John's Gospel, an interaction between John the Baptist and Jesus that beautifully illustrates the operation of the Holy Spirit:

> The next day he [John the Baptist] saw Jesus coming toward him, and said, 'Behold, the Lamb of God, who takes away the sin of the world! This is he of whom I said, "After me comes a man who ranks before me, because he was before me." I myself did not know him, but for this purpose I came baptizing with water, that he might be revealed to Israel.'[24]

John the Baptist goes on to say, 'I saw the Spirit descend from heaven like a dove, and it remained on him. I myself did not know him, but he who sent me to baptize with water said to me, "He on whom you see the Spirit descend and remain, this is he who baptizes with the Holy Spirit."'[25]

John the Baptist was in the middle of baptising people when Jesus turned up. But the interesting thing is that the passage says he didn't know who Jesus was. He doesn't know Him naturally as the Lamb of God, but he is able to point Him out and says, 'Behold, the Lamb of God'. How does he do that if, as the Bible says, he doesn't know who Jesus is? The answer is that John knows the Holy Spirit.

John was the last of the prophets of the old covenant. And as a prophet he operated by the word of the Lord. Although he didn't know Jesus as the Lamb of God, he knew the Holy Spirit. In the Old Testament, prophets were known as 'seers', because they 'saw' in the Spirit. He saw the Spirit descending on Jesus and he heard God's voice. This happens a lot among the Old Testament prophets. They say things like, 'the word of the Lord came to me, saying'. So they audibly heard the word of the Lord or saw the work of the Lord.

Here is John the Baptist saying that the same one that spoke to him to baptise people is now saying, 'Here's the one who baptises in the Holy Spirit.' In fact John is saying three things:

1. Here is the Lamb of God who takes away the sin of the world.
2. Here is the one who baptises in the Holy Spirit.
3. Here is the Son of God.

It's an interesting order. You can't have number two without number one. You can't be baptised in the Holy Spirit without being born again first. And once the first two take place, there's an increased revelation of number three – who Jesus is. He's God's Son. And as God's Son, through His death and resurrection, He makes a way for us to know the Father. It's a complete deal. It's done. Jesus' death on a cross, His breaking of the power of sin, death and sickness as He died and rose again means, as Jesus said on the cross, 'It is finished'.[26]

That 'finishing' is our starting. Being saved, full of the Holy Spirit and being sure as to who Jesus is means we are ready to move on in God's power. Our relationship with God is complete. There's nothing in the way. We have that same power Paul talked about.[27] First, we accept the Lamb of God. Second, we get baptised in the Spirit. Third, we begin to see the Son of God actively at work in our lives as we pray and minister to others in the power of and in partnership with the Spirit.

Paul prays for 'the Spirit of wisdom and revelation, so that [we] may know him better'.[28] That Spirit, that baptism in the Spirit, means we know Him. We know Jesus better. We are confident as we minister because we *know* Him! We *know* He is the Son of God.

We can *know* that when we are filled with the Spirit, there comes a holy dimension of revelation – God begins to reveal things to us. Revelation comes into our Christian life. We can expect it. We hear the voice of God; we become alert to the things of the Spirit. When we really begin to see the greatness and the fullness of who Jesus is and what He has done, it changes the way we operate. We *know* Him. So when we pray for someone, we *know* with what authority we are praying. As believers we have a real authority to pray for healing, to speak to the enemy and command him to leave. Why? Because we are saved, filled with the Holy Spirit and *know* Him.

Acting on the truth

A few years ago, following the leading of the Holy Spirit to do so, I invited a friend of mine, an ordained minister, to join myself and our team on a mission to a particular region of India. Although he had attended Bible school for four years and been officially ordained in his denomination, he had only recently been baptised in the Spirit, and had never experienced signs and wonders first-hand. One afternoon, while I was preparing in a back room for what would be a large open-air gospel campaign, two deaf and dumb girls turned up at the house where I was staying and asked the Indian pastors if they could receive prayer from me. Not wanting to disturb me, the pastors turned them down. However, my friend turned up at the house just as they were about to leave and, on discovering the situation, offered to pray for them. He later told me that he wanted to act on the truths he had been learning in the morning leadership seminars about how to move with the Holy Spirit and exercise authority in the name of Jesus. He prayed every prayer he could think of, but nothing seemed to work. Finally, while pausing for breath, something happened that had never happened to him before. He heard a voice inside him say, 'It's a deaf and dumb spirit!' Wanting to do the right thing, he mentally checked biblical references to ensure Jesus had cast out such spirits in His ministry, and once satisfied that it was the biblical thing to do to proceed, he commanded the deaf and dumb spirits to come out of the girls. Within moments the two girls were released and started to joyfully praise God and went off down the road happily talking to each other, having received a miracle from Jesus by the power of the Holy Spirit.

You may feel inadequate, lacking in experience or training, but if you're a believer in Jesus Christ, filled with the Holy Spirit, you can do what Jesus did in His name. He is calling you into a life of adventure in the kingdom of God. A life of miracles. A power partnership with the Holy Spirit.

Endnotes

1. Romans 8:11
2. Galatians 3:1-3 (NIV)
3. Galatians 3:5
4. Luke 9: 1-6
5. Luke 10:3 (NIV)

6. Luke 10:18-19 (ESV)

7. Luke 10:21 (for example, KJV; NIV)

8. 1 John 4:4

9. Dr Martyn Lloyd-Jones, *The Christian Warfare: An Exposition of Ephesians* 6:10-13 (Edinburgh: Banner of Truth, 1976), p280

10. Ephesians 1:19

11. Mark 10:15

12. John, chapters 14–16

13. (NASB)

14. See Luke 24:49

15. Luke 11:9-13

16. John 7:37-39 (NIV)

17. Galatians 5:25

18. For example, John 14:16

19. Galatians 5:16

20. Acts 1:8

21. John 7:37-39

22. Acts 1:8 (NKJV)

23. Acts 2:17

24. John 1:29-31 (ESV)

25. John 1:32-33 (ESV)

26. John 19:30 (ESV)

27. Romans 8:11

28. Ephesians 1:17 (NIV)

Chapter Two:
What the Bible Says

We are going to dig some more into what we've been learning. When we begin to understand what the Bible says, our faith increases. In fact, faith comes by hearing the Word of God. And when our faith increases, so does our boldness! We have an increased awareness of the authority we have in Christ.[29]

It's so important we *understand* what God has done through baptism in the Holy Spirit, rather than just experience the baptism as a one-off event. That's because the baptism in the Holy Spirit is a gateway to all the different gifts of the Spirit – as we will discover in these pages.

It's also important to understand that the term 'baptism in the Holy Spirit' is an entirely biblical one. In years past, there have been occasions when some churches and Christian organisations have suggested that the whole experience of the baptism in the Holy Spirit is something in the past – often they will argue that the baptism has been replaced by the Word; the Holy Spirit baptism replaced by the Bible. That's simply not true, and not in the Bible! There are no texts that can back that up in any meaningful way. But as we will see, there are many texts that point clearly to a life-changing baptism in the Spirit.

One thing you will notice with someone who argues against the baptism is that they don't say it's 'not real' – simply that it's 'not for this present age'. That's because the Bible is full of stories of the work of the Holy Spirit and of people being baptised in, and filled with, the Holy Spirit. So no one can argue from a 'not real' point of view; they tend rather to argue from a 'no longer relevant for our age' position.

As we have already seen and will see through these chapters, the Bible speaks loud and clear as to the relevance of the baptism of the Holy Spirit in our present age. Quite apart from that, however, we have to ask the question that if Jesus Christ, the Word of God made flesh, needed to be baptised in the Spirit to be effective in His ministry[30] and the apostles, who gave us the New Testament under the inspiration of the Holy Spirit, all needed the power of the Spirit in their ministries,[31] how much more do we? We, who are preaching Jesus' teaching and the apostles' teaching today, need that same ministry of the Spirit in our day as they did in theirs if we are going to bear the same fruit for God's kingdom that they did.

Are we not called to walk as Jesus did?[32] And are we not called to minister as He did?[33] If so, surely we cannot do that authentically without the same spiritual power that He had? Thank God the power of the Holy Spirit is as relevant and available today as it ever has been!

Faith from the Word

God's Word shows how relevant the baptism is. We read story after story of miracles and healing. We see again and again how God moves in power through Jesus, His disciples and through ordinary people. One of my favourite stories is of the paralysed man brought to Jesus by his friends, who made a hole in the ceiling and lowered him down.[34] I'm not sure what the house owner would have thought of that kind of destruction, but it's clear the man's friends were expecting a miracle!

Scripture tells us that 'the power of the Lord was with [Jesus] to heal'.[35] There was a particular anointing that day. The Pharisees were offended and the people around were amazed, saying, 'We have seen extraordinary things today.'[36]

We have a God who does extraordinary things! The proof is there, in the Word of God.

There is a faith that you get simply by reading the Word of God on any subject in the Scriptures. But if you meditate on it sufficiently, you begin to *hear* the Word and it will cause faith to arise in you. Allow God's Spirit to stir you – even now as you are reading this.

That's my challenge for you. Read the Word with regard to baptism in the Holy Spirit. Read the stories of Jesus healing and of the early apostles in the book of Acts. Ask God to encourage you through His Spirit as you read – and He will. You will find that as you read of healings and miracles, faith arises within you. After all, we are the same as those early apostles! We live under the same sun. We have the same Holy Spirit. We have that given authority from Christ.[37] Plan to read regularly from the stories in the Gospels and Acts relating to healing, miracles and salvation – and as you do, faith will arise within you.

Early in my ministry, I faced the issue of what the Word said and how I needed to respond.

I was in Rwanda on one of my first visits. Aged just twenty, I was a bit of a novice, but was passionate for the gospel. In the meetings, we had seen hundreds of salvations and a few people being healed, but really nothing worth writing home about in terms of greater healing miracles. Then, during a walk in the community, a woman pushed through the crowd and tried to grab hold of me, screaming at me. She was a witch and was out to curse me. I shook her off. Later on, I saw her again in the distance and decided to confront her. As I ran towards her, I was shouting out to her, commanding her to stop in Jesus' name. And then, in front of my eyes, she disappeared.

I was disturbed by the whole episode. Back at the hotel, I called home and asked the church to pray. As I prayed myself, I felt God drawing me to Acts chapter 3 in the Bible. It tells of John and Peter healing the cripple in Jesus' name at the temple gates and then declaring Jesus' supremacy to the people. I then heard the Holy Spirit say to me, 'Never forget who you are, and who you represent!' I had first stepped out in my teen years in evangelism and miracles, believing the words I had heard a preacher speak: 'You are who God says you are, and you can do what He says you can do.' Now again, the Holy Spirit was giving me a strong reminder to embrace and stand in who I was in Christ and believe in the authority of the One I represented. The Word came alive to me and my faith level grew.

That evening at the meeting, I moved out in my new-found faith and the results were glorious! Many came to a saving faith and there were lots of people healed. One woman came to the front of the meeting. Her face was shining as she pushed through the crowd and told of how God took away her blindness that night as she physically saw Jesus standing in front of her. As I had prayed over the crowd, a sensation of heat had gone through her body and her eyes had been opened.

And God opened my eyes that night as well. I saw, through the inspiration of the Word, the power and authority we have in Christ. I was no longer fearful of the enemy's tactics and instead, spurred on by the Word, saw God break through the strongholds the enemy had established in people's lives.

Remember who you are and who you represent!

The gateway

Baptism in the Holy Spirit is a gateway to the other gifts of the Holy Spirit. So it's important to understand exactly what we are talking about if we want all that God promises us in His Word.

Sometimes you hear people say that rather than 'baptism' in the Holy Spirit, a better term might be a 'filling' of the Spirit.

They argue that 'baptism in the Holy Spirit' is a Pentecostal term, used primarily by the Pentecostal Church. Well, it certainly is a term used by the Pentecostal Church, but baptism in the Holy Spirit is a fully biblical term. We read of it right at the beginning of the book of Acts, right at the beginning of the Church's story.[38] It is included in the book of Hebrews as a foundational doctrine of the Christian life. Here's the verse:

> Therefore, leaving the discussion of the elementary principles of Christ, let us go on to perfection, not laying again the foundation of repentance from dead works and of faith toward God, of the doctrine of baptisms, of laying on of hands, of resurrection of the dead, and of eternal judgment.[39]

There are some interesting items in this fundamental list of doctrines, and there in the middle of the passage is 'the doctrine of baptisms'. The word 'baptisms' is clearly written in the plural, and the writer is referring to baptisms that include baptism in water and baptism in the Holy Spirit. For this to be listed as a fundamental doctrine is telling. The writer is keen for us to understand that this doctrine is a principle of the Christian faith. Without the baptism in the Holy Spirit, we are operating below God's intended level. We are without a fundamental part of all God has intended for us.

This shows itself in the story of Philip in Samaria. He's an evangelist and many were finding faith in Christ, and had even been baptised in water – but without an accompanying baptism in the Holy Spirit. Clearly the apostles in Jerusalem, who trained under Jesus, felt that there was more needed at the start of these new believers' lives. It took Peter and John's visit to sort things out and ensure that the new believers were not to remain below God's intended level of operation in this world.[40] Baptism in the Spirit is God's gateway into a life lived in the power of the Spirit and operating in the gifts of the Spirit. To function as a Christian without the power of the Holy Spirit is to be less than God intended.

The body of Christ

We read this in Paul's letter to the Corinthians:

> For just as the body is one and has many members, and all the members of the body, though many, are one body, so it is with Christ. For in one Spirit we were all baptized into one body – Jews or Greeks, slaves or free – and all were made to drink of one Spirit.[41]

Paul is writing to the young church at Corinth, and he is reminding them that when they received Jesus as Saviour and Lord, they were baptised *into* the body of Christ. The Greek word is *baptiso*. It means to 'submerge into', to 'immerse'. This word is used to remind the believers that when they received Christ they became part of His body, His Church. It is to remind them that they are not alone, and they have a function to fulfil in serving and building up that body. But the same word is used about baptism in water and baptism in the Holy Spirit. In other words, God wants every believer to recognise they are baptised into Christ, and thus also into His Church. Their old identity in sin is dead, and they are raised to newness of life in Christ, and are called as part of His Church, to be immersed in the power of the Holy Spirit. They are to operate together to change the world we live in, as authentic witnesses to the risen Jesus, knowing the full anointing of His Spirit, enjoying a power partnership. That full anointing is to be seen in our church gatherings, our daily lives, and out onto the streets and public places of our nation.

New creation life

At the beginning of time, God breathed. He breathed on man and life was created.[42] Now consider this: when Jesus arose from the dead, He appeared to His disciples. It's a key moment in the resurrection story. This is what the Bible says:

> On the evening of that day, the first day of the week, the doors being locked where the disciples were for fear of the Jews, Jesus came and stood among them and said to them, 'Peace be with you.' When he had said this, he showed them his hands and his side. Then the disciples were glad when they saw the Lord. Jesus said to them again, 'Peace be with you. As the Father has sent me, even so I am sending you.' And when he had said this, he breathed on them and said to them, 'Receive the Holy Spirit.[']'[43]

Just as at the beginning of time, God breathed; so now God, through Christ, breathes. Jesus breathes on the disciples and says, 'Receive the Holy Spirit.'

At the beginning of time, God breathed on Adam and he received life. And so again with Jesus, the last Adam, He breathes again. Again life is received. Jesus is the end of the old Adamic order and He's the beginning of the new creation of God. He's 'the firstborn from the dead'.[44] And in beginning the new creation of God, He begins in exactly the same way as the first creation started. He breathes. He breathes on the disciples, and they are born again.

What a moment! How amazing! God breathed at the start of creation and breathes again at the start of the Church. Paul says this very thing to the Church in Corinth; that 'it is written, "The first man Adam became a living being"; the last Adam became a life-giving spirit'.[45]

In this beautiful act, God is giving new creation life. But it's not yet the full baptism in the Spirit. Note that the disciples are instructed to remain in Jerusalem until the Holy Spirit comes.[46] Salvation comes first, then the baptism in the Holy Spirit.

Powerful living

How do you want to live? Do you want a life of power and fulfilment, or a life that is powerless? It's a rhetorical question, of course. Who would want to live a powerless, impotent life when there is a power for living that can transform both us and those we minister to?

One of the most famous stories in the Gospels is that of the woman from Samaria. Jesus tells her that the water He gives will become 'a spring of water welling up to eternal life'.[47] John, writing the Gospel, doesn't want us to be in any doubt as to what is meant. John goes on to say a few chapters later:

> On the last day of the feast, the great day, Jesus stood up and cried out, 'If anyone thirsts, let him come to me and drink. Whoever believes in me, as the Scripture has said, "Out of his heart will flow rivers of living water."' Now this he said about the Spirit, whom those who believed in him were to receive, for as yet the Spirit had not been given, because Jesus was not yet glorified.[48]

There it is again. The Bible is so clear on this, leaving us nowhere else to go in our thinking. There is a Holy Spirit empowering available for each of us, given once Jesus is glorified. In fact, John goes so far as to say the baptism in the Holy Spirit cannot be given until such time as He, Jesus, has gone back to the Father's side – a clear reference to Pentecost and the Holy Spirit falling upon the Church.

Jesus calls this baptism 'the promise of [the] Father', and a 'power from on high'.[49] Have you received this promise, this power? Are you ready to? Even if this means a change in theology, be encouraged to search the Scriptures for yourself. Look at those verses we have referenced. And as you do, be willing to change where you need to change. A change of mind now will allow a change of heart. A change of mind now will allow a Holy Spirit baptism that will bring an anointing and power to your life; a Holy Spirit baptism that will baptise you into God's purposes for you and impact many lives for the kingdom of God.

Four accounts

There are four accounts of believers being baptised in the Spirit in the book of Acts. These are breakthrough passages and we will look at each of them. They are as follows:

- Acts 2:1-4. Here is the first instance of baptism in the Spirit within the Church. It's the day of Pentecost; every believer is baptised with the Spirit, all speak in other tongues and this baptism transforms the disciples from being fearful to being bold.
- Acts 8:14-17. This is the account of Peter and John going down to the new believers in Samaria. They realised that these believers had not yet been baptised in the Holy Spirit, so they went ahead and prayed. The result was that all received the baptism in the Holy Spirit.
- Acts 10:44-46. As a result of a dream, Peter ends up at a Gentile's[50] house. As Peter preaches, God works by the Holy Spirit, and while he is still preaching, all are baptised in the Spirit and speak in other tongues.
- Acts 19:1-6. This is the story of Paul finding out that the believers at Ephesus had not heard of the Holy Spirit. The Bible makes it so plain that this is a needed baptism and in

this story, the Ephesian believers are immediately baptised in the Spirit when Paul lays hands on them, and they speak in tongues and prophesy.

The precursor to the filling of the Holy Spirit at Pentecost, our first breakthrough passage, is Jesus' appearing to the disciples just before He ascends to heaven. It's recorded in the Gospel of Luke, and we looked at it earlier. This is what Jesus says:

I am sending the promise of my Father upon you. But stay in the city until you are clothed with power from on high.[51]

The Greek word used in this passage is *dunamis*. It is translated as 'power' here, but is also translated elsewhere in the Bible as 'mighty works' or 'miracles'. So Jesus is saying, 'Wait, you're going to be clothed with power, with an ability to do mighty works, with an ability to perform miracles.' That's the promise. And that's *our* promise! A life of miracles for every believer.

As we read each of these four passages in the book of Acts, we can – and should – read them with an application towards us. When we are baptised in the Spirit, we are operating under a *dunamis* power to heal, to be effective witnesses to Christ and the gospel, to work miracles, to do mighty works in Jesus' name. And yes, as some would rightfully remind us, even to live with the available power to be martyrs for Christ, should we ever be called upon to make that ultimate sacrifice. (The Greek word for 'witnesses' in Acts can be translated as 'martyrs').[52]

As Peter and John operated in Christ's authority to baptise others in the Holy Spirit, so can we. As Paul lays hands on others, so can we. As we read of the many healings in the book of Acts, we can operate in that same way. As Peter had dreams which affected his ministry, so can we.

Let's be ready, anticipating the promptings of the Holy Spirit to move out in power and authority, to operate in the same *dunamis* power as those early apostles. In nearly fifty nations during the last thirty years, I and my team have seen literally thousands of 'ordinary' believers in Christ receive the baptism in the Holy Spirit, step out in simple faith and move in miracles, the gifts of the Spirit, and lead people to Christ. It is the inheritance of every believer, and that includes you![53]

Power and compassion

The Church worldwide is known for its compassion. The whole world applauds as we work for the poor, as we help to set women free from prostitution, as we build schools and dig wells. These things are exactly what the Church should be doing. But that's not all. For some local churches, though, it *is* all. That's *all* the Church does.

But if compassion is as far as we go, we fall short of God's call upon the Church. We are called to radically change the world we live in. Yes, through compassion. But also through a *dunamis* anointing that heals the sick, opens blind eyes; even raises the dead. And unashamedly preaches the gospel.

Dunamis is the same root Greek word from which we get the words 'dynamite' and 'dynamic'. This *dunamis* is far more than a work of compassion. There's spiritual dynamite at work. God intends that we explode onto the scene in works of power.

When John the Baptist suddenly begins to doubt who Jesus is, he sends his disciples to Jesus to ask if He is the One. John doubts because of his situation. He's in prison. He can't see anything beyond the four walls of the cell. So it's an important question for John: 'Are you the one…?'

And what does Jesus say? He tells John's disciples to go back and report what they see:

And Jesus answered them, 'Go and tell John what you hear and see: the blind receive their sight and the lame walk, lepers are cleansed and the deaf hear, and the dead are raised up, and the poor have good news preached to them.[']⁵⁴

With due respect to the compassion ministries in the Church, Jesus does *not* say, 'the schools are built and the wells are dug'. In fact, His reference to the poor is not in terms of compassion but in terms of the gospel being preached.

The Church needs to work in the area of compassion. But we must not lose sight of the fact that when Jesus was moved with compassion He healed the sick.⁵⁵ We must respond to God's call – the main call on our lives – to live and proclaim the good news of Jesus in the *dunamis* power of the Holy Spirit and to demonstrate His love in signs, wonders and miracles!

There's the challenge. That's what the Bible says. Are you ready to respond?

Endnotes

29. Romans 10:17
30. Luke 3:21-22; 4:1,14; Acts 10:38
31. Acts 2:1-4, Acts 9:17
32. 1 John 2:6
33. John 14:12; Matthew 28:18-20
34. Luke 5:17-26
35. Luke 5:17 (ESV)
36. Luke 5:26 (ESV)
37. Matthew 28:18-20
38. Acts 1:5
39. Hebrews 6:1-2 (NKJV)
40. Acts 8:14-17
41. 1 Corinthians 12:12-13 (ESV)
42. Genesis 2:7
43. John 20:19-22 (ESV)
44. Colossians 1:18 (ESV)
45. 1 Corinthians 15:45 (ESV)

46. Luke 24:49
47. John 4:13-14 (NIV)
48. John 7:37-39 (ESV)
49. Luke 24:49 (ESV)
50. A Gentile is a non-Jewish person
51. Luke 24:49 (ESV)
52. Acts 1:8
53. John 14:12
54. Matthew 11:1-5 (ESV)
55. Matthew 14:14

Chapter Three:
Living it Out

God has spoken to you. The Bible confirms it. So don't wait. Don't delay. You've read this far (thank you!), so you must be keen to see God move more in your life. And there's nothing stopping that from happening.

When Jesus ministered on the earth, He laid aside His heavenly privileges[56] and ministered as a man. That's why He needed the Holy Spirit to come upon Him. You can read it in the gospel of Luke.[57] The Holy Spirit comes upon Jesus at His baptism. Up to that point in His life, He has done no miracles, but from that point on, the miracles flow. Why? Throughout His earthly life, Jesus is both the Son of God and the Son of Man, but for the miracles to flow through His ministry as the Son of Man, He needs the power of the Spirit. As we all do. Jesus is the pattern for every believer, and we are to walk in His footsteps.[58]

Don't wait

Following the Holy Spirit coming upon Him, Jesus is led out into the wilderness,[59] and there He defeats the devil by the word of God in His mouth. Note the order! Filling of the Spirit first. Defeat of the enemy second. You want to live a powerful, overcoming kind of life? Don't wait. Get full of the Holy Spirit. And learn to fill your mouth with the Word of God – use it as a powerful weapon against the enemy.[60]

Having defeated the devil in the wilderness, the next thing we read is Jesus entering the synagogue at Nazareth:

And he came to Nazareth, where he had been brought up. And as was his custom, He went to the synagogue on the Sabbath day, and He stood up to read. And the scroll of the prophet Isaiah was given to him. He unrolled the scroll and found the place where it was written,

'The Spirit of the Lord is upon me, because he has anointed me to proclaim good news to the poor. He has sent me to proclaim liberty to the captives and recovering of sight to the blind, to set at liberty those who are oppressed, to proclaim the year of the Lord's favour.'

And he rolled up the scroll and gave it back to the attendant and sat down. And the eyes of all in the synagogue were fixed on him. And he began to say to them, 'Today this Scripture has been fulfilled in your hearing.'[61]

Opening the eyes of the blind. Setting the captives free. Proclaiming the year of the Lord's favour. You can't do these things without the power of the Spirit.

Jesus, filled with the Spirit, declares the scripture fulfilled. You and I, filled with the Spirit, can declare the same. The Spirit of the Lord is indeed upon us to proclaim good news, to set the captive free, to literally give sight to the blind. That's our call! That's our destiny! The Son of God was also the Son of Man. He broke the devil's hold on you and me. He broke the chains of death. He rose from the dead. And He sent the Holy Spirit!

Don't wait any longer. God's got a calling on your life He wants to fulfil!

And don't tarry either!

I was at a conference. Sat next to me was a lovely Ghanaian pastor. He was an evangelist and church planter, and had been for many years. As he heard the talk that day on the power of the

Holy Spirit, he leaned over to me and said, 'I've been tarrying for fourteen years now for this power of the Spirit.'

What was he saying? He was using King James Bible English to say he was still waiting for the baptism of the Holy Spirit; tarrying, just as Peter and the 120 disciples had been told to do by Jesus in the upper room, before Pentecost.[62]

But what my friend was forgetting is that Pentecost has come. There's no need to 'tarry'! In fact, if you want to use that verse, you really have to get on a flight to Israel as it says to wait in Jerusalem! Clearly that's not what the verse is saying. It's telling us the story of the coming of the Holy Spirit in power at Pentecost for all people. But He's come! There's no waiting needed. No tarrying!

I said to the Ghanaian pastor, 'Goodness me, brother, I could have saved you fourteen years!' I continued, 'I'm not boasting, that's not the point, but look – Jesus only said once, "Tarry in the city of Jerusalem until you receive power from on high." That time has come and gone. The Holy Spirit has come. There's no need to wait any longer. Can I pray with you?'

He smiled. We found a quiet corner at the conference and this lovely man found a new power that day to help him in evangelism and church planting.

Don't wait. And don't tarry either!

Get desperate

The one thing I can say about this charming Ghanaian brother is that he was so thirsty. And of course, if we want to receive the Holy Spirit, this is a prerequisite. You've got to be saved and you've got to be thirsty.

I barely laid my hands on my pastor friend. I said, 'Receive the Holy Spirit.' When I did that, he just started speaking in tongues – and wouldn't stop! He went on for four hours. I left him after half an hour. I thought, 'I'll leave him there and see him after dinner.' But he wasn't at dinner! He was away, praying in tongues.

He went back to Ghana, and last I heard, he had planted many new churches – and he just keeps going and going and going! He's on fire. It's the power of the Spirit.

We read just after one of those four breakthrough passages in Acts that a certain former sorcerer was so desperate for the Holy Spirit, he was willing to pay![63] You can't buy the Holy Spirit, of course. But if you are desperate for God to move, you qualify.

The importance of tongues

We'll look at the gift of speaking in tongues in detail later on. But just to say here – this gift is so important! Often, it is the first manifestation of the baptism in the Holy Spirit.

Our next breakthrough passage in Acts shows us this.[64] Peter is at Cornelius' house – and there's no one more surprised than Peter! He hadn't understood Jesus' words about going into the entire world.[65] He hadn't understood this included the rest of the world beyond the Jews. And God showed him this first through a vision, and then through speaking in tongues. After the Holy Spirit fell on everyone while Peter was preaching, they all started speaking in tongues, and Peter says:

Can anyone withhold water for baptizing these people, who have received the Holy Spirit just as we have?[66]

Peter recognises that God has clearly accepted these non-Jews, justifying them through faith, and has poured out His Holy Spirit on them. On what basis did he conclude that God had received them just as He had received and saved believing Jews? '[T]hey heard them speak with [other] tongues.'[67] Speaking in tongues is a clear identifier to baptism in the Holy Spirit.

Some theologians over the years have suggested that tongues – speaking in, and interpretation of – is the least important of the gifts because it's at the end of Paul's list of gifts of the Spirit in his first letter to the Corinthians, chapter 12.[68] But by that logic, self-control would be the least important fruit of the Spirit,[69] and of the three things that Paul particularly highlights as remaining throughout time and eternity,[70] love would be of less importance than faith and hope... because it's at the end of the list! But Paul goes on to say it's the greatest of the three. Of course, being bottom of the list, meaning it is of less value, is not true for the fruit of the Spirit – nor can it be so for the list of the gifts of the Spirit.

Don't let the past rob you

When I go to a church that does not believe in the gifts of the Holy Spirit, I will sometimes provoke them to reconsider their position. I ask them to read 1 Corinthians 14:1. This is what it says:

Pursue love, and earnestly desire the spiritual gifts, especially that you may prophesy.[71]

I ask the congregation whether they are obeying Paul's instructions to pursue love.

'Yes,' they say.

'So how about the rest of the verse?' I ask.

Silence.

'Well,' I say to the pastor, 'you appear to have a bunch of rebels in your church! There is selective obedience going on here!'

If we follow Paul's instructions, we should not only pursue love but prophecy (and the other gifts) as well. We can't pursue one without the other.

In the last of our breakthrough passages in Acts, we read of

Paul asking the believers in Ephesus whether they received the Holy Spirit when they believed.[72] It's a loaded question! It turns out that the believers there had an incomplete deal. They had only been baptised into John's baptism and had no understanding of the Holy Spirit.

It's plain to read from each of the four breakthrough passages in Acts that it's possible to miss out on the baptism of the Holy Spirit. We need that baptism to operate in the power that God intends for us. Anything less is less than God's best for us.

I was at a Christian dinner when one of the hosts started loudly to speak against the need to be baptised in the Holy Spirit. He was accusing the whole of the charismatic Church of leaving their thinking outside the church door. Well, God has a way of sorting these things out! During the meal, the Lord gave me a word of knowledge for someone at the meal. I shared that God had said to me there was someone present that had damage to the third vertebrae of the spine, resulting in a really bad back. It turned out to be the wife of the man that had been speaking badly of the charismatic Church that responded!

As his wife was instantly healed while we prayed, the man was gracious enough to apologise. He admitted that he used to be a Pentecostal and had been baptised in the Spirit but that he had been verbally hurt by others in the church and had gone away from his original theology as a result.

If you're reading this now, and have been hurt in some way by others in the Church, forgive them! Don't let these things fester. Don't let these things in the past rob you of God's best for your life today.

Waiting to be perfect

There can be a tendency as Christians to believe that somehow through holy living or reading the Bible we can earn the baptism of the Holy Spirit in our lives. While all good and godly practices are beneficial, we can't lay claim to God's blessings on the grounds of our performance. The Holy Spirit is the promise of the Father – a genuine gift in every way.

One time I was ministering in a Baptist church in Serbia. It was the tenth night of the mission there. We were all pretty tired by now; especially my interpreter, who had been translating everything right through the mission.

It was a cold night outside – as low as -29°C! The heating in the church building was doing its best to cope.

Early on in the meeting, a tall man in his twenties came in and sat near the front. I hadn't seen him before, but assumed he was an 'on fire' believer as he sat so near the front.

As I was preaching, my very tired interpreter was beginning to get things wrong. Every now and again, the tall young man would interrupt and correct the translation. 'No,' he would say, 'it's not that word, it's this word…' This happened quite a few times.

Eventually, my interpreter got a bit fed up with it, spoke in Serbian to the young man, and they exchanged positions. My new interpreter was fantastic! He translated so accurately, and with real feeling. When I raised my voice, he raised his voice. When I whispered, so did he. When I jumped up and down, so did he!

It was a great meeting. God was clearly at work through the Holy Spirit and there were a number of words of knowledge for people – accurately identifying issues in people's lives supernaturally.

Then we got to the 'altar call'. I always invite people to receive Christ at every meeting I do. You never know who is there.

I said, 'If anyone wants to come to Christ tonight, you can pray a prayer right now, and God will change your whole life!' My translator was silent, so I said it again. 'If anyone wants to come to Christ tonight…'

The young man just looked at me. Then he spoke: 'Can I… can I do that?'

'What do you mean?'

'Can I give my life to Jesus?'

'I… I don't understand. I thought you were a Christian. I assumed you were already saved.'

'No. This is my first time in church. I came in to get out of the cold!'

So, with the church praying with me, we led the tall young man to Christ. I said to him, 'You know, you can be filled with the Holy Spirit as well. You can have all I've been talking about tonight. Some people wait for years to be baptised in the Holy Spirit, but there's no need to wait.'

I prayed some more. He began to speak in tongues. It was an amazing time.

Then I began to minster to the sick, with my young friend continuing to interpret. We got to one lady who clearly had one leg shorter than the other. We prayed and the leg visibly grew. I said to my newly saved interpreter, 'Why don't you pray for the next person?'

'Really?'

'Yes, why not? It's about a God who heals, it's not to do with the number of years someone has been a Christian!'

The young man began to pray for a man who was deaf in one ear. And there in the meeting, the man began to hear! The young man was astonished.

The church leaders told me what happened next. The young man went back home that night and immediately led his wife to Christ. What an amazing God we have.

He's the same for you too. Too many of us are waiting for the day we are perfect. That's not a day that will happen this side of eternity! The thing is, you don't have to wait to be perfect to receive the baptism in the Holy Spirit. You don't have to be perfect before you start moving out in the power of the Spirit. The blood of Jesus has made you righteous in God's sight, and He is ready to fill you, to use you the moment you become a Christian. As we've seen, the Bible says that's the truth. Begin to live it out. Don't wait. Don't tarry. Get desperate. Don't let the past rob you and don't wait to be perfect.

Why not ask right now for a refilling of the Holy Spirit? Why not begin to ask God to help you to step out in praying for people, and in beginning to use the gifts of the Spirit? It's time to step up to God's call on your life and live it out.

Endnotes

56. Philippians 2:5-11
57. Luke 3:21-22
58. 1 John 2:6
59. Luke 4:1
60. Ephesians 6:17
61. Luke 4:16-21 (ESV)
62. Luke 24:49; Acts 1:4-5
63. Acts 8:18-19
64. Acts 10
65. Matthew 28:18-20
66. Acts 10:47 (ESV)
67. Acts 10:46 (KJV)
68. 1 Corinthians 12:10
69. Galatians 5:22-23
70. 1 Corinthians 13:13
71. 1 Corinthians 14:1 (ESV)
72. Acts 19:1-6

Chapter Four:
Engage with God

We've been learning how to start living out what God has done in us. We've seen that there's nothing stopping us moving in the power of the Spirit. We're ready to go; ready to engage.

Baptism in the Spirit is a doorway to engaging with God on a deeper level; a doorway to living out the life God always intended for us. It's an empowerment to be effective witnesses for Christ and build up the body of Christ as we move in His gifts.

Little anointed ones

The term 'Christian' was intended by enemies of Christianity as a term of abuse. It was used in the early days of the Church in the city of Antioch to describe Christ-followers. Calling them 'Christians' was calling them 'little-Christs', or 'little anointed ones'. I don't know about you, but I'm happy to take that insult. That's what we are – little anointed ones. Through Christ, through the baptism in the Holy Spirit, we have the same anointing. We may be little – but we are anointed too!

We have a new identity. In fact, we are completely new! It's not that Jesus has renewed the old Jonathan Conrathe – He has not! Jesus didn't want to renew the old sinful Jonathan, He wanted to put that old sinful self to death so that I could live in newness of life. My old life is gone! We don't try to resurrect our old life; we live in the good of the new life God has given us. That's what Paul means in Ephesians when he talks of us putting on the new self:

Put off your old self ... be made new in the attitude of your minds ... put on the new self, created to be like God in true righteousness and holiness.[73]

We have a brand new life. That's encouraging, isn't it? A whole new life.

And that's why we are 'Christians'; little anointed ones.

Righteous

We are anointed ones – and we are righteous.[74] Although it is a totally biblical word, 'righteous' can be seen as a bit of a 'religious' word to some – and it certainly needs explanation. We are, of course, not talking about 'self-righteousness' here, but rather what the Bible describes as the '*gift* of righteousness',[75] given to everyone who believes in Jesus. It means that we are 'made right' through Christ's death on the cross. Justified. Declared 'not guilty' by God Himself, through our faith in Christ. We have a 'new self'. As such we can approach our holy God and know we are accepted. We are righteous. Christ has taken our sins, and imputed to us His righteousness. A divine exchange has taken place – and it is the very essence of the gospel.

Until we really understand this, we can't actually move on to live in the Spirit, because we would be living a life that is preoccupied with our old self. We would be forever trying to sort out our old life instead of engaging with God and living in the good of the new life.

I'm not opposed to ministry and counselling – a lot of us have been through some pretty messy stuff in our lives and it's good to get it sorted. But remember we are living in the new life; we have a new self. In fact, we are unable to live as Christ intends if we don't develop a right attitude as to what has gone before. Ultimately, we all have to make a decision to repent of things past, forgiving those who have sinned against us and our loved ones, turn from our own sins, and put our faith in Jesus and what He has done for us. We must wholeheartedly believe who God declares we are in Christ as the truth, regardless of our feelings. Many believers are hampered with a sense of guilt or shame because of their past sins, and sometimes for sins they may still be struggling with as they walk out their new life in Christ and start to grow in holy living. We will dedicate more time to 'walking in the Spirit' as we go through this book, which is the key to victorious Christian living as we embrace the grace of God and His gift of righteousness. But for now, please understand that living under condemnation is not the Father's will for your life. In fact, Paul says that 'there is now *no* condemnation for those who are in Christ Jesus'.[76] Understanding this principle is right at the doorway to the Spirit-filled and Spirit-led life. The writer to the Hebrews urges us to grow in our understanding of 'the word of righteousness', stating that if we don't, we stay in a state of perpetual spiritual babyhood, unable to embrace a lifestyle of sensitivity to the Holy Spirit and a growth in godliness.[77]

The alternative to embracing God's gracious gift of 'no condemnation' is less than God's best, because trying to sort out our old self is a dead end. If that becomes our reality, with the kingdom of self and the kingdom of Satan being so closely intertwined, we get into trouble. The enemy will always have you looking out for the next thing that needs sorting out. You will always be dealing with failure, rather than rejoicing that Christ has made you righteous. When the Holy Spirit is at work in our lives and we are yielding to Him and moving forward, it's amazing how much stuff gets sorted out along the journey.

I see this so often on mission. We regularly take people on mission both in the UK and around the world. It's amazing what gets sorted when you are on the frontline! When you are focused on Jesus, and His mission, perhaps faced with a witchdoctor in Uganda, or a gang planning to beat you up on the wrong side of a British town, to use more extreme examples, you start to lean on God for your protection. You are calling on Him to help you, to answer you. In the process you draw close to Him, your first love, and so many of the wrong thoughts, attitudes and habits of your past start falling away from you. Those issues that were taking your house group leader or pastor hours to sort out are… sorted out! They are just gone! When you serve on the frontline, reaching out to God, He draws near to you. In that drawing near, transformation takes place.

It's healthy to look outward and not to be constantly looking inward. It's great to realise we don't have to be spiritually crippled and bound up, living our lives 'in the rear-view mirror'! We can actually deal with something quickly, turn the focus away from our self and towards what is out there for us in the purposes of God. And what is out there are other people's lives. Lives that need Christ. Lives that most certainly are more of a mess than most of ours were. When we realise we are enabled and can make a difference in people's lives, the old self shrivels up. God takes the weak[78] and he uses them as little anointed ones; as little Christs, to change this world.

Small acts of obedience

The theologian and scholar Eugene Peterson talks about a long obedience in the same direction.[79] What he means is walking our walk a step at a time, always in the same direction, towards Christ. Each step on our journey is a small act of obedience. And as we step forward, God meets us. He uses us in His purposes. We sense His presence and power.

When we get up on a Monday morning, we may not feel particularly 'spiritual'. We may not feel we have God's Holy Spirit anointing on us. But the reality is that He is always with us, and will never leave us or forsake us.[80] His anointing abides in us[81] and as we get up, choosing to praise Him, pray, read the Word and ask God to help us in our workplace, home or school, then He who is everywhere (omnipresent), whether felt or not, is manifested personally to us and we are filled and strengthened. And by small acts of obedience throughout the day, we are working with Him. Working with Him in the power of the Spirit. We can and must learn how to cooperate, to partner with Him in the day-to-day if we are going to live a life of miracles. But it's great to know that even when we don't feel we are doing that well, He is still with us, and upon us, moving in our lives, and the potential of Him moving powerfully through us is only one small step away as we learn to listen and obey His gentle promptings in daily life.

Without those small acts, it's possible to go for a whole day without any real experiential knowledge of God with us. But, as we take small steps, God meets us, helps us in that difficult meeting at work, encourages us in the challenges of relationships and family life, and brings healing, peace and salvation in our day-to-day mission to reveal Christ to the world.

As we learn to listen and take small steps of faith, worked out in small acts of obedience, His power is manifested in us through the Holy Spirit. And in particular, God gives us gifts of the Holy Spirit to help us.

On one occasion after a twelve-hour journey in an old beaten-up Eastern European car, all the way from Serbia to the Czech Republic in scorching temperatures, the Holy Spirit spoke gently to me, in a quiet inner voice, telling me that He wanted me to go into the factory opposite the garage where we had stopped to get the car repaired and to minister healing to all those who were suffering in their backs and joints. To cut a long story short, after going in to meet the managing director, who got instantly healed of a long-standing whiplash neck injury and subsequently gave her life to Christ, I was given access to the workers. Following a brief introduction by the managing director and with the help of my interpreter, I preached the gospel and prayed for the sick. Every one of the factory workers was instantly healed and half of them gave their lives to Jesus. Learning to hear and obey the gentle promptings of the Holy Spirit, to do what we see the Father doing,[82] is key to the release of miracles and seeing many turn to Christ for salvation. Great breakthroughs follow small acts of obedience.

Understanding the gifts

1 Corinthians chapter 12 lists a number of gifts of the Spirit.[83] These are gifts given to us as believers to use, in partnership with the Holy Spirit, on a daily basis. While they are to be used to build up the body of Christ on both a personal relationship level and in church gatherings, they are certainly not limited to those expressions. They are for us to use and minister to others, both to the body of Christ, and to the world around us as acts of His mercy, revelation and power that flows as we step out in faith-filled obedience to the Holy Spirit. The gifts are listed as follows:

- Word of wisdom
- Word of knowledge
- Gift of faith
- Gifts of healings
- Working of miracles
- Prophecy
- Discerning of spirits
- Speaking in tongues
- Interpretation of tongues

Very broadly, we can break down these nine gifts into three groups of three. Firstly there are the proclamation gifts – speaking in tongues, interpretation of tongues and prophecy. These are the gifts that *say something*. We make use of these gifts to declare and proclaim the word of God to both believers and to those not yet Christians. They can be used in the context of speaking to those with or without a Christian faith.

Secondly, there are the revelation gifts – these gifts *reveal something*. They are the word of wisdom, the word of knowledge and the discerning of spirits. These are breakthrough gifts in the sense that God will show us what is happening in someone's life, in a situation or in the spiritual world, and give us wisdom to know what to do about it, often using us to speak into something with Holy Spirit-inspired knowledge and insight. This opens up opportunities for God to bring great breakthroughs.

Thirdly, there are the power gifts – these are the gifts that *do something*. The gift of faith, gifts of healings and the working of miracles. Each gift has a profound effect on the person receiving them. They involve healing, creative miracles and manifestations of a measure of God's faith and 'special faith' for a particular situation. It is God working in power.

In the following chapters, we are going to look at all three groups in turn.

All the gifts all of the time

First, I want to make clear that as Christians we have access to *all* the gifts of the Holy Spirit. While it is true that God does give certain distinct ministries to certain individuals in the body of Christ,   we need to be careful that we do not waste too much time trying to find out which gift of the Holy Spirit has been given to us. The answer is, *all* of them! In one sense every one of us has every gift. After all, in terms of ownership they are His gifts, not ours. But in terms of stewardship, they are ours to ask for, to stir up, to step out in faith for. The Holy Spirit is within us and all the gifts are inherent within the Spirit. And as we start stepping out in the gifts, serving the body of Christ with these gifts of grace, and reaching out to the world, we discover areas where God has particularly anointed us to minister. But it is always important to remember that it is never intended by God for them to be exclusive, as if you were limited to that expression of gifting, but rather that that area is a 'grace specialism' for you, in the midst of the other gifts of the Spirit that remain available for you to access, as for every other believer.

What is the best gift? The answer is, whatever gift is most suitable to the situation we are in. No gift is more important than another. The gifts of the Spirit are there for us in the circumstances we find ourselves in.

Yes, it's possible that we have more faith for the operation of one particular gift of the Spirit, but don't limit yourself to that. 'I'm sorry, I can't pray for your healing – God has only given me the gift of words of knowledge.' What a nonsense that would be. There are seasons when we seem to be operating more in one gift than another, and that's fine. But seasons and circumstances change. The gifts are there for us – as gifts from God for us to minister to others. Don't limit yourselves!

Stepping out

How do we operate in these gifts? We get filled and stay filled with the Holy Spirit. We learn to listen to those quiet inner promptings, that knowledge, those impressions or pictures that He gives us, and step out in faith. Remember we discussed the small acts of obedience? Really, operating in the gifts of the Spirit is exactly that. We step out, and often on the first thing He shows us. We may not feel we have faith for a situation, but we will find that as we step out in obedience, God meets us there. After all, real faith is not a feeling, it's an action.[85]

Jesus, speaking in the Gospel of Mark,[86] says that signs will accompany people who believe. The Greek for 'believe' means to exercise actual faith, not just to have general faith as a Christian. We step out. We do what Jesus did. We pray for the sick, cleanse those with leprosy, drive out demons, preach to the multitudes, and yes, even raise the dead. Once we have done that we can start to think about what gifts God has given us as particular ministry gifts!

Some people try to work out what their gift is before they activate any faith to start moving. That's the wrong approach. You start moving – and that releases faith and grace. It's a whole lot easier to redirect a car that is moving than try to redirect one that is stationary with the handbrake on. God is a God of faith and He responds to our steps of faith, however small they may appear.

Faith excites the Holy Spirit

When I worked with the evangelist Don Double (very much my mentor in my early ministry years), he used to say that faith excites the Holy Spirit. That's a great statement! Don would regularly throw me in at the deep end and watch me swim. In many meetings he would just announce to the congregation that I had a word of knowledge for them. I felt as if I had no such thing! At first when Don did this, I'd go over and whisper to him that I had no words of knowledge; that he must have misunderstood me. But Don would say that he had not misunderstood anything, that there was always something if I would just reach out for it. Then he would send me to the microphone to reach out for 'that word', which I did with every bit of faith I could muster.

The most amazing things happened each time I approached the microphone. A word of knowledge as clear as anything would come. It happened again and again... sometimes as an impression, sometimes as an internal picture, or a feeling in my body that corresponded with a condition in someone else's. I became very aware that Don may decide to call on me at any time. And that meant that my prayer life was strong! I didn't want to get caught out. I spent a lot of time, hours in fact, praying in tongues, because I had realised by then that this gift so often released the revelation and power I so desperately wanted and needed to minister. Quite apart from the fact that I really didn't want to be standing at that microphone with nothing to say!

How about you? Are you ready to step out? Pray regularly in tongues. Be prepared for God's promptings. The words are there if we reach out for them. When a word comes it lifts faith, and when faith is raised it releases power and then the gifts of the Spirit get released more actively.

L plates

A lot of the reason for our nerves when we begin to engage with God like this comes down to our own insecurities. We feel we can't afford to make a mistake. What would people think of us? But God is smiling. He loves us stepping out in faith and is not offended if we get it wrong. We need to remember that throughout our Christian lives, we are constantly wearing L plates.

Just because the first time we reverse around a corner when we learn to drive, we go up onto the pavement, doesn't mean that we give up driving. We keep driving.

From the moment we leave our mother's womb, we begin to learn. We grow. We learn to walk. We lean to talk. We study. We pass exams. There is a constant learning. It's why you are reading this book – you want to continue to learn.

When we are first filled with the Holy Spirit, we are learning. Just as we began to learn from the day we came out of our mother's womb, so too we begin to learn the day we step out in this new realm of the Spirit. That's exactly what Jesus did when He walked on this earth. The Bible says He did what He saw the Father doing.[87] He listened to and depended on His heavenly Father, acting in perfect faith upon what His Father showed Him, and miracles poured out from Him to meet the desperate needs of broken humanity. He invites us to learn of Him, to walk in step with His Spirit, and partake of His miracle life to reach our world today in a power partnership with the Holy Spirit.

Results

What results can we expect as we wear our L plates and step out? We can genuinely expect to see the same kind of miracles that Jesus and the apostles moved in as recorded in the Gospels and Acts. However, while sometimes it's powerful healing or creative miracles that we see, sometimes God just wants to minister gently and tenderly into the brokenness of someone's life. Let me tell you a story which I hope will encourage you.

I was teaching at a local church over a weekend and in the last meeting God took me by surprise. It was near the end of the meeting and there had been a wonderful time of ministry. The Holy Spirit had moved in such a way that many were flat out on the floor. Others were standing with hands raised.

That's when I saw her. A lady in her early forties was standing there with hands raised. I felt God was speaking to me in some way about her hands. Just then the pastor came over. Noticing that I was looking at this lady, he spoke to me.

'Jonathan, I do hope you can help her. She has a problem with obsessive cleanliness. She is forever washing her hands. It happens every few minutes. It has got so bad and has been so disruptive in the family that the husband feels he has no choice but to leave her. We have prayed for her, counselled her, given many hours of our time to help her, but nothing seems to have happened.'

I walked over to the lady, asking God to speak to me. At moments like that in ministry, it's often as if I am looking through God's eyes. You can pray like that. You can ask God to speak to you just by looking at someone.

I was aware that the last thing this lady needed was yet more ministry and counselling. As I was looking I felt God prompt me just to speak the words of John's Gospel: 'You are already clean because of the word I have spoken to you.'[88]

I leaned forward and whispered into her ear, 'You are clean already.'

That was it. Not the most profound of words. But I could see immediately the impact of those words. God began to move by His Spirit and for the next forty minutes or so she was laughing and crying before the Lord.

I caught up with her again, with her husband and children, about three months later. She said, 'Since that time, since you spoke those words over me, I have never washed in that obsessive manner again. Everything has come into balance; I am completely free from years of obsession from that one moment.'

God is good.

And that's the point. God is good! He so wants to speak into people's hearts. He is ready to minister and to transform lives.

Are we ready to listen; to look at situations as the Holy Spirit looks at them? Are we ready to take those small steps of obedience and see what God will do? If we do, a lifetime of adventure in the kingdom of God awaits us as we walk with Jesus, ministering in the love and power of the Holy Spirit.

Endnotes
73. Ephesians 4:22-24 (NIV)
74. 2 Corinthians 5:21

75. Romans 5:17 (NIV; author italics)
76. Romans 8:1 (NIV, author italics)
77. Hebrews 5:12-14 (ESV)
78. 1 Corinthians 1:27
79. Peterson: *A Long Obedience in the Same Direction*, IVP, 1980
80. Matthew 28:20; Hebrews 13:5
81. 1 John 2:20
82. John 5:19,30
83. 1 Corinthians 12:1-11
84. 1 Corinthians 12:28-31
85. James 2:17
86. Mark 16:17
87. John 5:19,30
88. John 15:3 (NIV)

Chapter Five:
The Proclamation Gifts:
Tongues and Interpretation

We're going to look at each of the gifts of the Spirit over these next chapters. As you read these words, my prayer is there will be an application. That God will speak to you, encourage you, and as a result, you will engage with Him through the Holy Spirit and begin those small steps of obedience, using the various gifts of the Spirit as God directs.

Speaking in tongues

It's important to remember that the gifts of the Spirit are grace gifts. Paul talks of the gifts in his first letter to the Corinthians. He describes the gifts as 'grace gifts'.[89] That's the best interpretation of the Greek word he uses: *charismata*. The root word of *charismata* is *charis*, which is 'grace'.

This is so important as we look at the gift of speaking in tongues. This is a grace gift from God. It's not something we can work up. It is a gift.

Having said it is a gift, it was the disciples on the day of Pentecost that did the speaking when they were filled with the Holy Spirit. And Paul teaches us that we can pray in the Spirit at will, in the same way that we can pray with our mind at will.[90] Clearly this is a partnership, not a takeover! God has called us to cooperate with His Spirit in faith as we speak in other tongues. God's Spirit is given on the basis of a promise,[91] and we can act on that promise. It took me three years before I was personally released in speaking in other tongues after being initially prayed for to receive the baptism in the Holy Spirit, primarily because no one told me that I should just open my mouth in faith and start to speak, trusting God to give me a language other than my normal native tongue. When I did, the 'rivers' that Jesus promised in John chapter 7 began to flow, and have never stopped since that day!

We've already looked at the gift of speaking in tongues as being an evidence of baptism in the Spirit; and indeed it is. It's not the only evidence – Jesus promises 'power' when the Holy Spirit comes upon us.[92] But the stories in Acts[93] when people are filled with the Spirit and immediately speak in tongues are instructive as to the immediacy of the gift upon being baptised in the Spirit.

Intercession partnership

Perhaps surprisingly, bearing in mind the way tongues are used in the stories in Acts, speaking in tongues is used a lot for intercession. Here's what Paul says:

> The Spirit helps us in our weakness. For we do not know what to pray for as we ought, but the Spirit himself intercedes for us with groanings too deep for words. And he who searches hearts knows what is the mind of the Spirit, because the Spirit intercedes for the saints …[94]

We will each be faced with situations in life where we simply don't know what to pray for. That's when the Holy Spirit helps us with words that are too deep for intelligible speech. We cry out to God – there's a groaning within us for God to move. There's no way we can pray in our own language, simply because the words are not enough. We are engaging with God, crying out to Him to move. That needs speaking in tongues!

I first learned this 'kingdom secret' when I was a teenager. One of my friends, who was really on fire for God, was becoming increasingly frustrated with his younger brother whom he shared a bedroom with, because his brother had gone away from the Lord, and any time my friend went to his room to pray or read the Bible, his brother would come in and turn on loud music and do everything he could to distract. I encouraged my friend to come round to our family home where he and I would pray about the situation. It was a Sunday afternoon, and we prayed our hearts out to God on the basis of His promises with everything we could think of in our normal English language, and then started praying in tongues. The Holy Spirit fell on us, empowering our prayers, and we found ourselves praying in tongues for two and a half hours. At the end of this, as if by following the hand of an invisible conductor, we both stopped simultaneously! We looked up at each other, and with deep inner assurance, said, 'It's done, isn't it?' This is what the old Methodists used to call 'praying through'. We thanked God for the answer, declaring the work done.

Two weeks later, on a Sunday afternoon, while my friend's family were all sitting talking in their lounge, his younger brother walked down the stairs into the lounge and announced, 'I'm getting baptised! I've had enough of sin. I'm so sorry, I've put you all through hell, but I want to get right with God and follow Jesus.'

Amazed at this sudden turnaround, his father asked him, 'This is wonderful news, but when did this sudden change of heart happen?'

His response? 'It was strange. Two weeks ago, about four o'clock on Sunday afternoon, something came all over me and I felt so convicted, I knew I had to get right with God.'

When did we finish praying for my friend's brother? At four o'clock on Sunday afternoon.

The Holy Spirit is our senior partner in prayer, who comes alongside us to help us when we invite Him to, and prays through us the perfect will of God for any given situation as we use our prayer language of tongues – and at times with groaning and tears.

There is a beautiful partnership taking place here. A partnership between us and the Holy Spirit. The Bible says the Holy Spirit comes alongside us[95] to help us. As I mentioned earlier, the Greek translation of the verse is that He is the *parakletos*, the 'Helper'. We can't do this on our own. We don't even know what to pray. So we cry out in tongues and we find we are in partnership with the Spirit. The famous evangelist Reinhard Bonnke says that 'God always works with workers and moves with movers, but He does not sit with sitters'.[96] As we 'work and move' in the Spirit, rising up to do something about each situation through Spirit-filled prayer and faith-filled action, God works with us, and miracles happen!

A tongues miracle

I took a team out to Uganda not long ago. Before we left, we got a prophetic word from a pastor in Slovakia that we were going to meet someone there, a doctor, sitting in a restaurant, who would invite us to go to pray in the local hospital and we were to know that this was God's intention for us, and as we went God would move powerfully in the hospital. Sure enough, on the first evening in the town, we met a Christian surgeon in the restaurant of the hotel where we were staying who was visiting the local hospital and doing some work there. He recognised we were Christians and asked if there was any possibility of us going in to the hospital to pray for the staff and patients.

I was busy in the conference we were running, but I sent out a team to the hospital. There were some good testimonies of healing and salvation that came from that visit, but the most challenging moment was when they were asked to pray for a young lady that appeared to have died. No one had checked the body and verified that she was dead, but as the team described it, she didn't appear to be breathing, her body was cold and the family were mourning. That seems like pretty good evidence.

The team simply didn't know what to pray. So they agreed together to each pray in tongues at the same time, for ten minutes or so. So off they went, each praying in tongues; on and on for about ten minutes.

In the end they stopped. Nothing had happened. The body still lay on the bed as it had before. The body was still cold and there appeared to be no breath in her. The family continued to mourn as the team returned to the main ward to continue to pray with other patients.

A few minutes later, one of the team heard a scream. It seemed to be coming from the side room where the body was. She ran back in. And there, in front of her eyes, was the dead woman – sitting up in bed!

When we work and move with God, God works and moves with us.

Tongues to help us

One of the most interesting aspects of speaking in tongues is the fact that it helps *us*. Paul, again writing to the Corinthians, says it 'edifies' us.[97] Other translations of the same passage say that tongues builds a person up[98] or strengthens them personally.[99]

How does this work? Why does speaking in tongues edify us or build us up? Bible commentators suggest that one reason is because speaking in tongues helps us to understand God's Word better. Tongues can't be understood by another man or woman, but it can be understood by God. The Indian pastor Rambabu[100] says it's like having a hotline to heaven that only God picks up![101] We cry to God, maybe interceding for something, or someone, and God hears and answers. That's what happened in the hospital in Uganda.

But God responds to speaking in tongues with His anointing as well. We sense a peace when we speak in tongues. We sense the Holy Spirit with us. So it's no surprise, then, that He brings revelation to us and we begin to understand God's Word in a fresh way.

When we speak in tongues, we get to speak on the phone only God picks up. We get to receive an increased anointing and refreshment in the Holy Spirit. We get our spiritual batteries recharged. I can personally testify that I do not know anyone with any significant prophetic or healing ministry who doesn't spend a considerable time speaking in other tongues. Such prayer in the Spirit brings spiritual breakthrough. Many ministers of the gospel testify to the power of speaking in other tongues.

I have had the privilege of sitting under Jackie Pullinger's ministry as she testified of her work in Hong Kong's Walled City, stating that it was as she learned to pray in tongues more that Triad gang members and prostitutes began to get saved, drug addicts delivered, and the sick healed. John G. Lake, a well-known Canadian-American leader in the Pentecostal movement in the early twentieth century, was so powerfully used of God in healing that more than half a million healings were reported in his ministry in South Africa between 1908 and 1913. He prayed in tongues for hours every day and said 'praying in tongues was the making of my ministry'.[102]

There are so many testimonies of this nature in the Christian world. We cannot ignore the power of God that is available through this simple gift of speaking in other tongues.

More than one

Sometimes people will get stuck on one tongue. It's a gift from God and we enjoy speaking with that tongue, that unknown language. But 'tongues' are plural, not singular! Why stop at one tongue when there are thousands out there? Why get familiar with one tongue so that it stops blessing us in the same way?

I came home one time from a mission, really exhausted. I collapsed in my study, and sprawled on the floor; I cried out to God for blessing. As I did so, I began to speak in a new tongue that I didn't recognise I had used at any time before. God met me in a beautiful way. The blessing of the new tongue 'edified' me in a special way. I felt enveloped in His love, refreshed and strengthened; spirit, soul and body.

But that wasn't the end of it. As I spoke in tongues, my faith rose and I heard God's voice. He downloaded to me a message for the next mission. In fact, not just one message; ten messages! One for each night of the new mission! More than that, I saw in the Spirit, the first meeting laid out in front of me. I saw faces, the clothes people were wearing – where they were sitting. God showed me what some of them were going through.

When I later got to that meeting, it was exactly as God had set out in the vision. I saw the faces, recognised the clothes, and was able to speak powerfully and prophetically to each of the issues they were facing and that God had revealed to me.

I continued to dream each night after that. And each night I saw in my dream the meeting I would be leading. I saw how the stage was laid out and I saw the people I would be speaking to. Sure enough, the next day at the mission, it was exactly as it was in the dream! I saw the people I had dreamed of and I saw them responding to God's word and being healed just as I had seen in the dream.

All this came about entirely because God gave me a new tongue to speak in.

You want a strong faith in God? You want a ministry that is effective? Speak in tongues in your own personal time as much as you can.

Tongues in evangelism

Paul, writing to the Corinthian church, says that tongues are a 'sign ... for unbelievers'.[103] They certainly were in the most surprising way, in the hospital in Uganda! However, Paul is referring to a quote from Isaiah,[104] indicating that those who do not believe will continue in their unbelief. In other words Paul is saying that tongues, because they can't be understood by the unbelieving listener, will impact them with the sense of being 'outside' of the community of faith. That's true, of course, if they don't respond with repentance and faith in Christ. Tongues will continue to leave that listener in their unbelief. By contrast, Paul says, prophecy is for the believer.[105] In other words, a prophetic word, accurately brought, can change an unbeliever to a believer because they understand and recognise that the words apply to them.

This can be a hard section of Scripture to understand, but this interpretation is the most commonly held view[106] and makes the most sense in terms of the overall passage. However, there are also times when God has given believers the ability to speak in a tongue that their listeners did understand, such as at Pentecost, which impacts the unsaved as a sign from heaven and, when coupled with the gospel, can lead to salvation.

Another way that speaking in tongues has a direct and powerful effect upon an unbeliever is when the spoken tongue in a public meeting is then interpreted into the local language that can be understood by the congregation – and by the person without faith. At that point, tongues become a powerful force in evangelism.

We discussed earlier the use of tongues in our own devotions, of the power of speaking in tongues and what this can do for our own faith level. This, to me, is still the key use for tongues. But tongues can also be spoken out in a meeting, provided that there is an interpretation of what is being said. Paul puts it this way:

> If any speak in a tongue, let there be only two or at most three, and each in turn, and let someone interpret. But if there is no one to interpret, let each of them keep silent in church and speak to himself and to God.[107]

In the case of interpreting a tongue, the meaning becomes suddenly clear as it is interpreted. This may often be through an internal picture, or 'knowing', possibly an impression or scripture that is brought to mind. Although speaking in tongues is speaking directly to God, as at Pentecost, when God was magnified in their own languages, the process of hearing what God is saying through a tongue operates in a similar way to a prophecy or a word of knowledge. It's the Holy Spirit speaking to the person, revealing to them something God wants them to know. And in the case of someone without faith, it can be the moment that they find faith as they believe the interpretation is speaking to them.

Snow

The word is 'interpretation', of course. That's important. It's not a direct 'translation'. First of all we are imperfect, so won't always get it right. Secondly, depending upon the situation, it's not always possible to be exact.

I remember one time when we were in Tanzania. My friend

and mentor Don Double was preaching. He quoted from the scripture, Isaiah 1:18, where the Lord says, 'your sins are like scarlet, they shall be as white as snow'.[108] But they don't have snow in Tanzania, except at the top of Kilimanjaro sometimes. So the problem was that they didn't have any word in their local language for 'snow'. Don would be preaching away and whenever he got to the word 'snow', there would be a problem. The interpreter wouldn't know what to do. There was a silence. Don would just repeat the phrase a little louder and wait for the interpretation which was not forthcoming! Then one of the leaders got an idea and he spoke for a long time. All the time, Don was wondering what was happening and why there could be such a debate about the word 'snow'. It seemed like the leader was almost preaching his own message! Finally the leader turned and stopped. He explained that they had no word for snow in their language so he had helped them to understand what Don was talking about. In the end, he explained, the Spirit gave him an illustration. He reinterpreted the scripture to them and told them that though their sins were red like scarlet, God will make them like the inside of a coconut!

It's a wonderful story, both of the leaders' inventiveness and the prompting of the Spirit – proving God really does have a sense of humour!

So, interpretation of tongues is not translation. Sometimes you can take a long amount of time to explain a single concept. And other times it's a very short interpretation for a longer section in tongues. Whatever its length, though, with interpretation, tongues can be used by the Holy Spirit to build the people of God up in their faith, or to convict someone and bring them to a living faith in Christ.

Endnotes

89. 1 Corinthians 1:4
90. 1 Corinthians 14:15
91. Acts 1:8
92. Acts 1:8 (NIV)
93. Acts 2:4; 10:46
94. Romans 8:26-27 (ESV)
95. John 14:16
96. http://www.azquotes.com/quote/617225 (accessed 14.8.17). See also Mark 16:20
97. 1 Corinthians 14:4 (NIV)
98. 1 Corinthians 14:4 (ESV)
99. 1 Corinthians 14:4 (NLT)
100. Founder and President, New Creation Ministries
101. Talk at KingsGate Community Church Peterborough, August 2009
102. Mike Bickle, *Growing in Prayer* (Lake Mary, FL: Charisma House, 2014), p168
103. 1 Corinthians 14:22 (NIV)
104. Isaiah 28:11-12
105. 1 Corinthians 14:22
106. F.F. Bruce, *The New Century Bible Commentary: I & II Corinthians* (London: Marshall, Morgan & Scott, 1971), pp132-134
107. 1 Corinthians 14:27-28 (ESV)
108. (NIV)

Chapter Six:
The Proclamation Gifts:
Prophecy

Bringing a prophetic word to a person or a situation is one of the main ways God speaks supernaturally, and it can have a powerful impact on the lives of individuals, churches and even nations. However, for some in the Church there has been much confusion about prophecy and it seems that this most precious gift has sometimes been misused in certain situations over the years. Therefore, before getting too deeply into how we cooperate with the Holy Spirit in the gift of prophecy, it would be good to lay down some biblical foundations in understanding what it is, and how we should serve effectively in this ministry.

First things first... prophecy is still alive and kicking! It's not something that has died out or something that God has somehow replaced. God is still a speaking God, and as sons and daughters of God through faith in Christ, we should expect to be led by the Holy Spirit[109] and to hear His voice.[110]

God is a speaking God

God knows everything. Scientists will never know as much as God knows. Of course, they think they do, but God knows everything. He knows and He speaks. He chooses to use us, imperfect as we are, to speak His words. And that's what we do when we prophesy. We are tapping in to the God who knows everything.

We have learned that God spoke prophetically throughout the Old Testament, primarily through prophets who had the 'word of the Lord' come to them, or 'saw' supernatural visions, which is why they were called 'seers'. And we have learned that God still speaks. Our baptism in the Holy Spirit brings us into a closer relationship with our God and enables us, should we choose to, to hear His voice – not just for ourselves, but for others too.

Prophetic preaching only?

Let's deal with a misunderstanding first. There has been teaching in the past that suggests that prophecy today is simply inspired teaching. This comes from the same conservative preaching that implies that the gifts of the Spirit are no more and have been replaced by the Bible. There's no biblical proof for the latter – nor is there for the former! Nowhere does Scripture indicate that prophecy is simply inspired teaching! That said, all prophecy and preaching is subject to the written Word of God. Scripture itself is the measurement by which all teaching and preaching and all supernatural experience is to be weighed and judged.

Preaching can be inspired, of course. Hopefully that's always the case. We need to listen to the Holy Spirit when we are preparing or delivering sermons, and learn to go with the flow of God in this new covenant ministry that the apostle Paul calls the ministry of the Spirit, reminding us that 'the letter kills, but the Spirit gives life'.[111] But the gift of prophecy is more than just preaching a 'prophetic message' to the Church or to the world. There simply is no proof in Scripture to suggest that this is all there is to the gift of prophecy.

What is prophecy?

If prophecy is not simply inspired preaching, what is it? We studied earlier the relationship we have and need to have with the Holy Spirit. In its simplest form, prophecy is an ability to hear what God is saying and then to convey those thoughts, words, visions or dreams to others, primarily through the vehicle of the spoken word, and at times, actions. And we must remember that whenever revelation from God is spoken or acted upon, the power of God is present to confirm it.

In a sense, the whole of Jesus' earthly ministry came out of a 'prophetic flow' in the Holy Spirit, since He only did what He 'saw' His Father doing,[112] following the instructions, visions and prompts that He received either in prayer before ministry or during the flow of ministry itself. It is fundamentally important that we remember He is the model for every Christian's life and ministry.[113] He has not commissioned us to walk in the unachievable, but has provided His Spirit that we might learn how to partner with Him in our role as co-heirs and co-workers, proclaiming and demonstrating the kingdom of God.

We must learn what it means in practice to be led by the Spirit, to develop sensitivity to His gentle promptings and leadings in our inner self, our spirit, where He has come to dwell. We are the temple of the living God, both corporately as His Church, and as individual members of the body of Christ. The writer to the Hebrews encourages us to have our senses exercised to discern what is 'right' and what is 'wrong'.[114] Since he is talking about training our senses, he is obviously not referring merely to the training of our minds in logical, objective scriptural argument, but is referring more to a spiritual sensitivity that is developed not only in the Scriptures but also in the secret place of worship and communion with God.

We can know the Spirit's mind.[115] When we are not so quick to speak, but wait for a moment on Him, His thoughts will arise in ours, often as scriptures, impressions, internal pictures or an inner 'knowing' concerning a situation or person. He will also give us revelation concerning the Scriptures, opening our understanding to truth. He has given us His Spirit so that we might 'know' the things given to us by God. This 'knowing' is an experiential thing. Adam 'knew' his wife, Eve.[116] That does not mean that he studied a PhD about her! In the same way, this 'knowledge' of God is a deep personal knowing of God, where He reveals Himself, His Word, His purpose to our hearts. Scripture says that 'no one knows the things of God except the Spirit of God'.[117] You could go to Bible school and not 'know' the things of God in the sense of personally experiencing Him, hearing from Him, and having Him reveal truth to you in a personal manner. But thank God, in this relationship we enjoy with Him that Jesus calls 'eternal life',[118] He has given us His Spirit so that we *can* really 'know' the things of God. Believers in Jesus are the only people in the world who truly have inside information! It is His Spirit in us, revealing everything we need to know.

We can also know His will in every matter and decision of life. Firstly, there is objectively the Word of God, the Bible. And at this point, it is important to stress again that the Scriptures are the 'measuring rod' of *all* spiritual experience or supernatural direction we might receive. The Holy Spirit *never* leads us outside the perimeters of Scripture. By that we mean both the overall consensus of Scripture on a matter (as opposed to an isolated verse) and the principles of Scripture. As an obvious example, the Holy Spirit would never tell you to lie, steal or commit adultery. He would never tell you to leave your wife to marry another woman. God honours the institution of marriage, which He created and loves. The Word and the Spirit agree. Always.

Through His Spirit, God has given us an internal warning system for times when we might be making choices that are contrary to His will for our lives. It's called His peace. The apostle Paul writes to the Colossians:

Let the peace of Christ [the inner calm of one who walks daily with Him] be the controlling factor in your hearts [deciding and settling questions that arise].[119]

Sometimes believers ask for prayer, saying, 'Please pray for me that I might have peace about this decision so that I can go forward.'

I always say, 'Stop right there! The fact that you are out of peace demonstrates that you are out of the will of God in this area or decision. Peace is the state of a believer walking in the will of God. If you lose your peace, something is wrong. Go back to where you lost it and you'll get back into the will of God for your life.'

All prophecy is subject to the Word of God and to the peace of God in your heart. It doesn't matter how anointed the individual is who prophesied to you. If what is said does not line up with the Word of God and the peace of God, confirming what you have already heard from God yourself, don't receive it! Give it back to God and walk on with Jesus.

The Holy Spirit has emotions too. He is, after all, a person. The third person of the Godhead. He expresses His presence in our lives through love, joy and peace.[120] This is the fruit of the Spirit; His character, including His emotions, and they can dictate to our emotions too as we live our lives full of the Spirit and yielded to Him. He can be grieved, and you may feel that grief if you do something against His will in your behaviour or relationships. You may feel unsettled inwardly listening to some forms of teaching. Listen to the Holy Spirit inside of you. On the other hand, He may release great joy in you, as when Jesus 'rejoiced in the Holy Spirit,'[121] after His disciples reported to Him all the miracles they did in His name. The Holy Spirit will lead you into all truth, into all 'reality' as God defines it. So let's live full of His presence and learn to depend on Him. He has great things ahead for us as we learn to walk in the Spirit.

The promise

We know the prophetic promise. Here it is:

> And in the last days it shall be, God declares, that I will pour out my Spirit on all flesh, and your sons and your daughters shall prophesy, and your young men shall see visions, and your old men shall dream dreams ...[122]

The quote is from Joel and is used by Peter to describe what God is doing at Pentecost as thousands are saved. God will continue to do the same throughout the Church age until Jesus returns. It's interesting to note how prophecy, visions and dreams are some of the primary manifestations associated with the end-time outpouring of the Holy Spirit.

Peter speaks in more detail on what prophecy is in one of his letters. He says that 'no prophecy was ever produced by the will of man, but men spoke from God as they were carried along by the Holy Spirit.'[123] That's a good translation. We are carried along by the Holy Spirit. There is a sense of being in the flow of the Spirit; in a strong current. Note that we cannot 'produce' prophecy. It's not sourced in human beings, but in God. However, we can make ourselves more available to the Holy Spirit to speak through us by stirring up the gifts of God within us,[124] especially speaking in tongues. We can 'set [our] minds on the things of the Spirit,'[125] as the apostle Paul says. I find it helpful to ask myself, 'What would the Lord say to this person, in this situation?' and often He brings a scripture to mind, or some picture or impression that is in line with the Word of God. Sometimes in worship God will speak in the stillness; Scripture tells us His presence inhabits our praise and worship.[126]

As we have seen already, we will never be 100 per cent accurate when we speak in the prophetic simply because we are not 100 per cent perfect,[127] but as we are immersed in the Spirit and in the Word of God, carried along by Him, this will ensure we become more and more accurate.

What we say needs to be tested, of course; in particular, it must be in line with God's Word[128] and expressed with His heart. Paul teaches the Church in Thessalonica that we are not to quench the Spirit and that we certainly should never despise prophecy – but that it has to be tested.[129]

Nowhere in Scripture is there a suggestion that prophecy is for the few or for leaders only. On the contrary, the scriptures we have just studied suggest that prophecy is for everyone. Prophets are mentioned in the five-fold ministry.[130] There are people called by God particularly into that ministry, and there are those who, through developing in the gift of prophecy through regular use, grow into having a ministry of prophesying, such as Philip's daughters.[131] Nonetheless, Paul tells us that we can *all* prophesy.[132] And that includes you and me.

We are called to prophesy! The promise is there – the Spirit is poured out onto all flesh. And the method is there – we immerse ourselves in the Spirit, primarily through praying or singing in the Spirit, building our faith through the Word of God and learning to listen to His voice. Let's add active faith to that and see what God can do through us. Whatever gift we receive from God, we can use it according to our faith,[133] and when we do step out in that faith, it grows, and so does the accuracy, depth and strength of the gift itself.

The biblical qualifications of prophecy

We've learned that the gifts of the Spirit are for every believer. And we've learned that everyone who is a believer should prophesy. So that means that the moment you were saved and filled with the Holy Spirit, you were qualified and equipped. That's the biblical qualification for prophecy. You're saved? Filled with the Spirit? You qualify!

There are occasions when a prophetic word is strongly directional and there are also those people that are particularly used in prophetic ministry. The Holy Spirit may tell us of things to come. But generally, much prophecy is more about affirmation and confirmation than it is about strong directional words. It is a powerful gift available for everyone and is primarily used for the building up of the Church. It is for encouragement:

> [T]he one who prophesies speaks to people for their upbuilding and encouragement and consolation.[134]

So let's recap. Are you saved? You are qualified. Are you baptised in the Spirit? You can prophesy. Can you hear God's voice? You're in the flow of the Spirit. Does the word encourage? Exhort? Comfort? It's prophecy.

You qualify.

Covet

Paul says that we are allowed to covet just one thing! This is the only time we can see in Scripture that coveting is allowed. It's in that same passage we've been studying in 1 Corinthians:

> Pursue love, and earnestly desire the spiritual gifts, especially that you may prophesy.[135]

In the English Standard Version of the Bible (above) it says to 'earnestly desire' the gifts. But the root Greek word is the same as 'to covet'. We can covet the gift of prophecy! And earnestly desiring – coveting something – makes you sensitive and attentive to it. It gives you focus.

It's important to want to prophesy. I've spoken to too many people that say something along the lines of, 'Oh, well, God will give me the gift if He wants to.' But actually, He's asking you to covet it, to want it so much that you can't do without it. There's no room for complacency here. Don't just vaguely ask – covet the gift! Cry out to God for it. As we learned in earlier chapters, if you want the Holy Spirit's power, including His gifts, you have to be thirsty for them.

Perhaps this is the very reason you may never have prophesied before. Maybe you have pretended it's not real. Maybe you have never really thought about it. But think now. Do you want to bless the Church? Do you want to bring encouragement? Do you want to build people up, to see them develop and grow in Christ? If so, it's time to drop the apathy, discard the wrong thinking, and cry out to God for more.

He is so ready to bless you; so ready to give you the gift of prophecy. Covet it; cry out for it and see what God will do.

I've had the privilege of raising the dead on a few occasions. I can tell you, it's no use approaching a dead body with an attitude that says, 'Oh, well, if God wants to do it, He will.' No! We have to be full of faith, expectant, crying out for God to move!

I remember preparing for a meeting one time. I was asking God what He wanted for this particular time. Then I heard Him speak to me and say, 'What do *you* want, Jon?'

I said, 'What do You mean?'

God spoke to me again: 'Jon, I always want to move in power. I always want to set people free. I always want to heal and deliver. That's what I want every time, in every meeting. Now, Jon, what do *you* want?'

What a challenge that was! The Lord was calling me into agreement with Him, into this partnership of power in order to release His will in that situation through me. That's a challenge for us all. What do we want? Do we covet the gifts of the Spirit? Are we ready to move in power? Are we crying out for God to move? Are we ready to step out in faith?

Informed faith

Faith is not a mystery. Faith is informed. Faith is based on the revealed will of God. Real faith begins where the will of God is known.

Suppose I were to say to you, 'Come over on Saturday and I will give you the keys to our family car and you can have it as your own.' The reality is that if I said that to you, you could come to me with confidence and ask for the keys – because I had revealed it to be my will. But if I didn't say that to you and you asked for the keys for my car, I'm unlikely to agree!

Real faith begins where the will of God is known.

It's the same with prophecy. Prophecy is informed. We can know the Holy Spirit. We can learn how He speaks and communicates to us. God does not want us to be ignorant of Him or His gifts. And we can hone our listening skills by reading Scripture, praying in tongues, and waiting on Him to sense His presence and hear His voice or gentle impressions in our hearts.

He is a faithful God and He wants us to learn to walk in the realm of the Spirit with Him. As we do, as we know Him better, we are more confident in speaking what God is saying. We are more confident with the prophecies that we bring.

God has given us the keys to the prophetic. We can approach Him in confidence, sure that He will give us what we ask:

And this is the confidence that we have towards him, that if we ask anything according to his will he hears us. And if we know that he hears us in whatever we ask, we know that we have the requests that we have asked of him.[136]

In the words of the apostle James, 'If any of you lacks wisdom, let him ask God, who gives generously to *all* without reproach, and it will be given him. But let him ask in faith, with no doubting ...'[137] James goes on to say that if we doubt we won't receive anything from the Lord. So we must learn to pray in faith, on the basis of His promises, and when He gives us a word, believe it! Speak it! And in my experience, when you act on the first thing He gives you, He sees you're faithful and gives you more. That's the walk of faith. We are also encouraged here to 'ask' of God, which in the original Greek means to get as close to God as possible and ask in no uncertain terms what you want from Him. This is not apologetic; it means to ask clearly and boldly. God is not a reserved Englishman, and He wants us to come 'boldly' to the throne of grace.[138]

All the mercy and grace we could ever need, including revelation and power, lies on the other side of 'ask'.

Like Jesus

As followers of Jesus, we need to live and minister like Him. In fact, the very 'spirit of prophecy' is 'the testimony of Jesus',[139] and all the gifts, including this one, should glorify Him.[140] The disciples followed Jesus, not just because He was a good man, but because He was the Son of God. As such, He exuded the very character and power of God. Filled with the Holy Spirit, He moved consistently in the miraculous. There was not a day in the life of the disciples when they weren't being challenged. They observed the way Jesus lived. They observed the way He interacted with the Holy Spirit in prayer and ministry. They observed His compassion and power.

To be like Jesus is not just to be 'nice'. It's to be filled with the Holy Spirit; to be operating in love, truth and power.

Jesus was love personified. He was also love expressed in power.

If we really want to authentically express Christ, if we really want to move in the gift of prophecy and the power of the Spirit, we have to have the fruit of the Spirit and the gifts of the Spirit. We have to have the character of Christ and the charisma of Christ. Anything less than that is an imperfect presentation of Jesus Christ in our world.

It can be easy, when there are dramatic demonstrations of revelation or power through an individual, for people to become more focused on the vessel through which a gift of God has been expressed than on the giver of that gift, Jesus Himself. Let's ensure that while we honour the grace of God in someone, we give the glory and praise to God alone, and also seek to demonstrate His love to those who are ministered to, treating them with respect. While faith releases the supply of the Spirit,[141] it works through love.[142] There have been times in my own ministry over the years when the Lord through the word of knowledge has revealed to me details about people's personal lives, inappropriate behaviour and so forth. In the context of dynamic meetings where God was moving in significant ways, it could have been tempting to deliver such words to individuals in public but, knowing that such exposure may have been destructive, the Lord has almost always reminded me that His heart in such situations is not primarily for demonstration but for restoration. It has been a relief and joy to see the Father restore such individuals in a more personal context, and most often with local leadership present for the sake of accountability from my side (because what I'm saying can be sensitive and may be inappropriate one-to-one), and for ongoing support and discipleship for the individual's sake. The gifts of God are always for His glory and the good of those to whom they are ministered.

Pictures and visions

I hope this chapter has stirred you to be more active in prophecy. Before we move on, let's be practical. God will often give us a prophetic word by speaking directly into our hearts through a quiet inner voice, vision, impression or scripture. But He uses all our senses, and one of the ways He speaks prophetically is through what we see.

God will sometimes use tangible, physical things that we look at. Psalm 42 is credited as a psalm of Korah. The commentators think it is a psalm that reflects David and the plight he was in. It is probable that David's flight from Absalom was the cause for this psalm. He is running away. We are told that he and his troops are tired and thirsty.[143] They are met by friends, and food and drink is provided. It's likely that waterfalls were there too, so when the psalmist talks of 'Deep [calling] to deep at the roar of your waterfalls,'[144] it's a real picture of a real event. The spiritual is reflected in the physical. As David is thankful for food and water, he is reflective of the spiritual depth and refreshing of God's Spirit, of God's goodness towards him. The psalm is the prophetic picture of that moment.

The Bible says creation declares God's glory.[145] When we walk in the countryside, it's no surprise that God will speak to us through its beauty. In that moment when we pause, look, consider, there is a window of time where we become conscious of Him, sensitive to what He is saying to us through what we may see around us or, indeed, within us as a prophetic picture or image. God said to Jeremiah, 'what do you see?'[146] He saw the branch of an almond tree. The scripture doesn't tell us whether he saw it physically or spiritually, as in a vision, but the illustration is interesting because the almond tree in horticulture is nicknamed 'the waker' because it is one of the earliest blossoming and fruit-bearing trees. The Lord then commended Jeremiah for what he had seen, saying, 'You have seen well, for I am watching over my word to perform it.'[147] Ask the Lord to open your 'eyes'; that is your spiritual eyes, to see what the Father is doing, and to open your 'ears' to hear what He is saying, and expect Him to do so. Visions and dreams are the language of the Holy Spirit.

An audible voice

More often I have found that God speaks through inner impressions, pictures, sometimes physical things, and always through Scripture. Something I see either in physical reality or I see it inwardly. Sometimes I will hear God's voice on the inside, prompting me to speak. He often gives me the start of the prophecy that I can use to launch out in faith. Then, of course, He gives the rest of the word. That's just how He works. Through faith.

By the way, while God is awesome, holy and to be honoured, He communicates with us in a way we can relate to. He doesn't speak to us in King James Bible English. The individual prophesying may prefer the King James as their favourite version of the Bible and therefore use that kind of language to communicate what they sense God saying, but God Himself does not necessarily speak in that mode of English. He doesn't boom out in a strange voice either. While we may feel the strength of the Holy Spirit rising up in us as we prophesy, and there is nothing inherently wrong with speaking loudly, we don't need to fall into the trap of thinking that 'volume equals power'! He speaks as we speak. Of course He does – He wants us to understand.

God does speak occasionally in an audible voice, though. It's not something I go looking for, and I wouldn't encourage you to either, but God has spoken in that way on occasion.

I was in Ghana one time preaching the gospel to a large open-air crowd, and the witchdoctor and his friends turned up. They started banging the 'death drums' and trying to distract the crowd, hanging a turkey upside down and shouting all manner of things at me. I was frustrated, and I sensed God's righteous anger. I publicly announced, 'Jesus is greater than the witchdoctor and He will demonstrate it tonight by healing the sick!' Suddenly, as we prayed over the crowd, the sick started to be healed, people were coming to Christ, and many testified to miracles as they were touched by the power of God. In the midst of all this a man was brought up onto the platform. He managed to side step the senior pastor who was checking the miracles, and I assumed he had been seen by one of the other pastors and had come to declare what God had done for him. I asked him to testify to the crowd. Speaking into the microphone, he said, 'I am blind.' He then repeated it and to rub it in said, 'I have been blind from birth.'

It dawned on me that this man was not one from the group the pastors had interviewed, but had been brought onto the stage by a friend. And here he was, telling the crowd he was blind. And here I was, having earlier declared that Jesus would do miracles that night to demonstrate He was greater than the witchdoctor! I wanted to keep the momentum of faith going. There was a quick inward prayer of 'Help!' at that moment, that's for sure!

It was then that I heard an audible voice. This wasn't a voice in my head, it sounded like an audible voice that came over my right shoulder. It was so clear I turned round to see if anyone was speaking behind me, but there was no one. I heard the voice say, 'Receive your sight.' That was it. Just the words, 'Receive your sight.' My faith expanded somewhat as I realised it was God's authoritative voice. So I repeated the phrase as I put my hands on the man's eyes, commanding, 'Receive your sight, in Jesus' name!' It was a simple and confident declaration. And there in front of me, his eyes instantly opened, and the crowd erupted with shouts of praise and excitement.

The man began to touch my face, with tears of joy in his eyes, saying in his local language, 'I can see, I can see! I can't believe it, I can see!' The witchdoctor and his friends packed away their drums and left the meeting. Many turned to Christ that night.

Peace as the umpire

I want to repeat an important qualification as regards prophecy. We really need to know the peace of God as we speak. We may 'see' a situation correctly but it may not be the right time to bring a word. There has to be an inner witness as we speak. There is a huge difference between being 'driven' and being 'led'. The Holy Spirit leads, He doesn't drive. His leading is compelling, not compulsive. If I had not known that inner peace and release of faith when dealing with the witchdoctor, it may have been unwise to push ahead in praying for the blind man in front of the crowd as I did. The audible voice was a help to me in being certain that what I was seeing was on God's agenda for that moment.

I'm a 'faith man' and always believe in ministering healing to the sick in obedience to Jesus' command to do so, but there are instantaneous miracles of healing and there are recoveries too. Jesus, who had the greatest success rate of instant healing in the history of the world, did what He 'saw' the Father doing.[148] There are times when sufferers press through in faith for healing as did the crowds pushing through to touch Jesus, and everyone got healed. There are times when we are in the flow of the Holy Spirit, following His leading to minister to individuals, as Jesus did, healing one among many at the pool of Bethesda.[149] There is more than one scriptural way of getting healed, but when the Holy Spirit is moving and leading, we need to move with Him.

It's the same with prophecy. There's more than one way. But we can listen to God's direction, sense what He is saying by the Holy Spirit, and step out in God's timing and with His direction.

Paul says 'let the peace of Christ rule in your hearts'.[150] When we are dealing with the prophetic, particularly with directional words that can change a person's life, we need wisdom – and peace.

Discernment

It's important to recognise that when we are ministering to someone through prophecy, which is a revelatory gift, other gifts of the Spirit often operate with it, especially the word of knowledge and discerning of spirits. We will look in more detail at these gifts in the following chapters, but briefly, these gifts provide Holy Spirit-given knowledge about a person or situation, and what is going on in the spiritual world. They are *not* prophecy. The word of knowledge and/or discerning of spirits may tell you what's happening in someone's life, and even what's in their heart, but the prophetic word reveals *what God says* about that situation, that individual or desire. Knowing the difference is vital, otherwise we can be in danger of prophesying someone's situation or desire back to them as the word of the Lord for their life and get them bound up in a world of disappointment or even deception. This is where always keeping the prophetic word subject to the straightforward truth of Scripture is so important for healthy practice in this area of ministry, so that it only produces wholesome fruit in people's lives, as God intends it to.

For the sake of illustration, on one occasion the Lord gave me a prophetic word for a pastor's wife in a leaders' meeting. But as

I approached her, she said, 'Please don't bring me a word; I can't cope with any more words.'

This caused me to be inquisitive. I asked her what words she had had. She explained that the last person to prophesy over her had told her she was in a deep, dark valley.

'That's not the word of the Lord!' I said.

'What do you mean?' the lady said. 'The woman who gave me the word was a very spiritual Christian counsellor, a minister at a Christian retreat centre. She said it was God's word to me.'

I explained, 'There's a difference between discerning where someone is at through a word of knowledge or discerning of spirits, and prophesying into that situation what God has to say about it. The lady that spoke to you correctly discerned where you were at – but then she left you there! That's not God's will for you! He wants you out of that valley!' This dear pastor's wife, who had gone through several really difficult years in ministry and was struggling to overcome depression, broke into tears of relief and joy as the truth set her free, and by the grace of God I was able to bring her a fresh word of encouragement for her and her husband concerning their faithfulness and the new season the Lord was taking them into. I'm glad to report that the word came to pass, their ministry turned around within a few short months, and their church is now a thriving, growing community of believers.

Remember what we said earlier – prophecy is meant to be encouraging! Paul told the Church in Colossae to ensure that their speech was 'always … gracious [and] seasoned with salt'.[151] That's a great starting point for bringing a prophetic word. Before we deliver any prophetic ministry, let's ensure we pause for a moment and check that what we are about to deliver fulfils biblical criteria, the Spirit witnesses to it in our hearts, and that we deliver it in love.

We can hear God audibly; we can hear His prompts in our heart. We can hear God speak prophetically through what we see around us. We can hear God speak as we read His Word. And as we prophesy, we aim for it to be encouraging, comforting and uplifting.

Be bold, step out in faith, and see how God meets us as we are obedient in bringing the prophetic word.

Endnotes

109. Romans 8:4
110. John 10:27
111. 2 Corinthians 3:6 (ESV)
112. John 5:19,30
113. 1 John 2:6
114. Hebrews 5:14 (KJV, NLT)
115. 1 Corinthians 2:9-16
116. See Genesis 4:1
117. 1 Corinthians 2:11 (NKJV)
118. John 3:16
119. Colossians 3:15 (Amplified)
120. Galatians 5:22
121. Luke 10:21 (ESV)
122. Acts 2:17 (ESV)
123. 2 Peter 1:21 (ESV)
124. 2 Timothy 1:6
125. Romans 8:5 (ESV)
126. See Psalm 22:3; Acts 13:1-4
127. 1 Corinthians 13:9
128. Isaiah 8:20
129. 1 Thessalonians 5:19-21
130. Ephesians 4:11
131. Acts 21:9
132. 1 Corinthians 14:31
133. Romans 12:3
134. 1 Corinthians 14:3 (ESV)
135. 1 Corinthians 14:1 (ESV)
136. 1 John 5:14-15 (ESV)
137. James 1:5-6 (ESV, author italics)
138. See Hebrews 4:16 (KJV)
139. Revelation 19:10 (ESV)

140. 1 Corinthians 12:3
141. Galatians 3:5
142. Galatians 5:6
143. 2 Samuel 17:27-29
144. Psalm 42:7 (ESV)
145. Psalm 19:1-6
146. Jeremiah 1:11 (ESV)
147. Jeremiah 1:12 (ESV)
148. John 5:19,30
149. John 5:1-9
150. Colossians 3:15 (ESV)
151. Colossians 4:6 (ESV)

Chapter Seven:
The Revelation Gifts:
Wisdom and Knowledge

We're moving on to the next three gifts of the Spirit, often described as the 'revelation gifts'. They are the word of wisdom, the word of knowledge and the discerning of spirits. They get called the 'revelation gifts' simply because that's what they are – gifts that *reveal something* and very often open a door for God to move in significant ways.

The realm of revelation

I want you to picture something; I want you to walk with me. We are, by God's grace, in heavenly places, walking towards the throne of God. There's an overpowering presence that means we can hardly stand, but we keep walking. We sense the goodness of God and His willingness to bless. We are aware we have access to all that God would have us own; all the gifts of the Spirit that will help both our own lives and the lives of others. I want you to see, as we walk, a door in the heavens marked 'Revelation'. Let's go through it together and see what God has for us.

This door of revelation opens up to a realm of previously hidden things. God is always revealing Himself to us. He wants us to know His heart, His innermost thoughts, to 'see' and 'hear' what He is doing, that we might cooperate with Him in bringing about His kingdom reign upon the earth through prayer and ministry. He is a revealing God. While it is true that we see the revelation of what He is like in the beauty of creation, in the redness of the sunset, in the vastness of the universe, God has revealed Himself most perfectly through His Word, the Scriptures, and in His Son, the Word made flesh, Jesus Christ. But God reveals Himself directly to us today as well, speaking to our hearts, prompting us, giving us visions and dreams. We can expect to be led by the Holy Spirit!

We have already discovered how God speaks to us and we are able as a result to reach out in faith and receive the gifts of tongues, the interpretation of tongues and prophecy. God also reveals Himself as the *all-knowing* God that He is, in words of knowledge and words of wisdom. And that is exactly what words of knowledge and wisdom are. They are small portions of God's 'all-knowledge', revealing details about people, places, situations, past, present or future, and God's wisdom providing 'keys' to know how to apply that knowledge, how to respond to a difficult question or situation, or unlock relational conflict or doors that appear closed to some furtherance of His kingdom.

Knowing the Holy Spirit

As we become more aware of the Holy Spirit in our lives, of His closeness to us, of the whispers of the Spirit, we begin to identify God speaking to us through words of knowledge and words of wisdom. They are there for us. In fact, the more we learn about this area of the Holy Spirit's ministry, the more we realise we have been receiving words of knowledge and wisdom for a while but just didn't realise that's what they were!

Let's read Acts chapter 2. Peter stands to speak to the crowds at Pentecost and says:

But this is what was uttered through the prophet Joel: 'And in the last days it shall be, God declares, that I will pour out my Spirit on all flesh, and your sons and your daughters shall prophesy, and your young men shall see visions, and your old men shall dream dreams.'[152]

This is the outpouring of the Holy Spirit that started at Pentecost and is still going strong. This is the revelation of God's Spirit and a declaration that revelatory knowledge is a key component of His outpouring. We read of prophecy, of dreams and of visions. We are in the realm of revelation here and as a direct result of hearing from God, of seeing what God is doing, we have revelation which we can then step out in and see the miraculous. Paul, writing in 1 Corinthians, tells us:

'No eye has seen, nor ear heard, nor the heart of man imagined, what God has prepared for those who love him' – these things God has revealed to us through the Spirit.[153]

God has revealed these things through the Spirit, and given us His Spirit so that we might *know* the things of God. It's the realm of revelation.

To experience this realm, we need to develop our relationship with the Holy Spirit. That's not head-knowledge; it's an *inner knowing*. As we stated before, the Bible tells us Adam *knew* his wife, Eve. That's not an intellectual knowledge; it doesn't mean he academically studied her. There was a close personal relationship; a union. It's the same when we talk about a relationship with God through the Holy Spirit. It's not an academic study. It's a personal relationship.

Knowing through the Word

One of the main ways we can *know* in this way is through the Word of God, the Bible. We can read the Bible with only our natural eyes or with our spirit. It needs to be the latter. Let what you read take you into a deeper relationship with the Holy Spirit. Start to commune and fellowship with the Spirit before you read, as you read, and after you read. It helps me to ask the Father to speak to me through His Holy Spirit before I start reading the Word, taking a bit of time to pray in tongues and worship Him. Then I read, communing with Him as I do, where a verse may lead me into prayer, confession, worship or thanksgiving. All of the words of the Bible are God-inspired.[154] They are Holy Spirit-filled words. The Spirit and the Word agree. There is no inconsistency in God. And so, every one of these words are a reflection of God's nature and His character; His purpose and His kingdom. His words contain multi-levels of truth and grace and are always fresh with life.

That means that the Spirit will never speak in a way that is inconsistent with the Bible. If we think we have heard something from God but it doesn't line up with Scripture, let me assure you, it wasn't God. God's Word is truth… the absolute measure against which all spiritual experience can and must be measured.

Revelation in Scripture is never an end in itself. These things were written that we might believe, and believing always leads to action! When God gives us revelation, it's not to tickle our ears; it's not to make us excited about the supernatural realm. It is because He wants us to speak; He wants to impart truth to us, and He wants to do something on earth through us. Some of us just get a little overexcited about supernatural knowledge. It's not an end in itself, so let's remember that. There has to be an outworking of that knowledge, either then or at a later date. It's not something that puffs us up as some sort of prophet, but something that reveals truth, that builds up, accomplishes kingdom purposes and glorifies God.

Sensitive to the Spirit

Words of knowledge can have a significant effect on a situation, but we need to be sensitive to the Spirit and to what the Spirit reveals to us.

At one meeting, I was praying for a young woman who had severe rheumatoid arthritis. Many had prayed for her, but there had been no improvement. As I prayed for her, she fell to the ground. It would have been easy to leave it there, and move on to pray for someone else, but I felt a prompting from the Holy Spirit that I needed to continue to pray, as nothing had happened regarding a shifting of the condition.

As I continued to pray, God began to reveal more. I saw a picture of her standing at the top of a set of stairs. She was heavily pregnant, and as I 'looked' into the vision I instinctively 'knew' that the baby was eight months old. Then I saw her falling down the stairs and the baby in her womb tragically died. It was a difficult vision to see, and to communicate. However, as I sensitively told her what I had seen and asked whether the vision made any sense to her, the response was immediate and dramatic. She began to wail uncontrollably. It turned out that she had indeed been carrying a baby when she fell, and had lost the baby as a result. She had never forgiven herself. As I led her in a prayer of release and forgiveness, the rheumatoid arthritis completely left her body.

The Holy Spirit will reveal 'keys' to unlock situations in people's lives when we ask Him. These words of knowledge are available for every believer who is full of the Holy Spirit and learns to ask, to inwardly sense or look, and to listen for what He is saying.

Jesus the prophet

In one sense, everything Jesus did, everything that is recorded in the Gospels, is prophetic. As we have said earlier, Jesus said

He did nothing of Himself – it was all to do with what He 'saw' the Father doing.[155] Consequently, He saw and heard and then obeyed the Father – He is the prophetic Jesus.

He has been before us in walking in revelation. It's His sacrifice on the cross that gives us access to the heavenly places,[156] that allows us to walk through the door of revelation into all that God has for us, and through us, for others.

When we learn to hear and see in the Spirit, as Jesus did, we have a major key to the miraculous. When we walk through the door and into the realm of revelation, the Spirit is ready to speak to us, to reveal things to us. Sometimes in dreams and visions. Sometimes audibly. Sometimes through gentle impressions. Often directly through the words of God we read in the Bible. He's always available, always ready to speak to us, always ready to reveal hidden things as we operate in the realm of revelation. Every one of us has this access. Every one of us can operate in words of wisdom and knowledge.

The spiritual world and the natural world are always interacting. As we stand in a church meeting, in a queue at Sainsbury's, or travel in our car to work, God is with us. The spiritual world is all around us. There are angels present, and demons too.

But there's nothing to fear. Through Christ we have overcome. Consequently, although we live on earth, we are seated in heaven. We live in heavenly places in Christ[157] and it is from that place of authority in Him we can operate in the supernatural power of the Holy Spirit.

Practically operating in wisdom and knowledge

We've identified that we can all operate in words of wisdom and knowledge. All the gifts of the Holy Spirit are in the Holy Spirit, in us, and He is always ready to speak and to move in power; now we're going to look at *how* to operate in these gifts.

Some of us are more intuitive than others. Some of us have better imaginations than others. It's a bit of a generalisation, but women tend to have a head start at operating in these gifts, as they are generally more intuitive than men. Many of us men tend to get caught in the intellectual, when God wants to speak to us often in picture form, or through other revelatory means, such as impressions or, as is often the case where healing is concerned, He gives a sense of something in or around a part of your body that corresponds with a condition in someone else's. We need to train ourselves to be more aware of how God is speaking through our senses.[158]

This difference between men and women has been highlighted quite often with me. My wife, Elaine, will ask the question, 'Jon, where are you?' I answer, 'I'm right here, darling!' But what Elaine means, of course, is where am I emotionally on something, not where am I actually physically standing at the moment I am questioned! In other words, where am I beyond my natural, physical state?

We move beyond the natural when we operate in words of wisdom and knowledge. Hopefully we are already allowing faith to rise as we read this chapter. God really can work through every one of us! We don't have to be a Bible scholar and read the whole of the New Testament in Greek before we qualify. We are qualified because of Christ, who has brought us into the realm of revelation.

The next time you pray for someone, ask for a revelatory picture; something that can open up the situation you are praying for. He promised that everyone who asks, receives.[159] It may be that God will show you a particular circumstance in the person's life in the past that has resulted in a current condition, for example. Or maybe you get a picture in your mind's eye. If it's not obvious as to how the picture applies, ask God for more. If you don't get more, it may be good to ask the person about the picture you are seeing. What may not make sense to you may be abundantly clear to them.

This is operating with the word of knowledge. God has gifted you with an insight, a picture, or a sense of what needs to be done. This is direct revelatory knowledge to help us open up situations we may face or maybe those of the people we are praying for.

In a healing meeting I was conducting, the Holy Spirit spoke to me in the middle of my preaching, inwardly saying to me, 'There are five people here with major back problems and I want to heal them.' I stopped preaching, announced what the Lord had said to me and asked those individuals to stand. All five stood. One after another were instantly healed as I laid hands on them. But when I laid hands on the fifth person, a young woman, I felt the anointing go into her, and come straight out again. I did this several times, each time feeling the anointing come straight back out of her lower spine into my hand. Finally, I turned to the Lord in my heart and said, 'Lord, what is going on here?'

I immediately heard, 'She has an unsaved boyfriend and is sleeping with him.' Sexual sin is a sin against one's own body[160] and can open a door to demonic oppression in one form or another. When I quietly challenged her about this, she confessed it was true, immediately repented, and following further laying on of hands, was instantly healed.

You may just sense an 'atmosphere' around someone. It may not be a picture as such, but just a feeling – for example, when you are praying for someone to be healed, you may sense an atmosphere around them of doubt or anger. Or as in the case above, the Lord may speak to you inwardly. That's God's revelation for you. Move in on that revelation, ask the person what they are feeling and what that revealed word or atmosphere means to them. You can then pray that through with them, and move on to pray for healing once that is sorted.

The word of knowledge

Jesus regularly worked with words of wisdom and knowledge. One of the best examples is with the woman at the well.[161] Jesus had just turned up in the heat of the day and He asked for a drink. He knew what He was doing. He knew that it wasn't usual for a Jewish man to ask a Samaritan woman for a drink. And He expected a reaction.

Jesus led the conversation on from actual water to living water. As the woman became interested, Jesus then asked her to call her husband. The Father had already revealed to Him that she had no husband, and that, in turn, opened the conversation further and led to the whole town believing in Christ.

Jesus could have started right in with the word of knowledge that the woman had no husband and that she had previously had five husbands. But that might have been a short conversation! She would have very likely run away. Jesus was using wisdom along with knowledge, developing the conversation to the point that He could reveal the word of knowledge and change the woman's (and the townspeople's) life. She saw that it was better to believe than it was to argue.

One time I was on a mission with a pastor who did not believe in the baptism of the Holy Spirit. We were walking around an estate and I walked on for a while on my own, praying and asking God for breakthrough. Whenever I go out doing street evangelism, I deliberately don't go in a hurry. I dial down, because I want to listen. Successful evangelism is not about getting rid of as many leaflets as possible, but winning souls. If I want to advertise an event, I can employ a company to do that for me by giving out loads of leaflets. But if I want to win souls, I need to get out there and see what God is doing.

As I walked around the estate, I noticed the pastor talking to a group of eight women. They were giving him a tough time.

Most were smoking and all were settling in for a long argument. I moved closer and listened in. All the time I was asking God to show me a way to engage with them that would get their attention.

As I was looking on, I saw one of the younger ladies in the group. Suddenly it was just as if I was looking at an X-ray. I saw her left shoulder, inflamed and in pain, with the pain running right through to her left arm. I was looking with my eyes, but it was as if God had given me spiritual eyes to see the real issue. It was there in a moment and gone again.

Now I had the information I needed to get the attention of all the ladies. But what to say? If I were just to say it straight away, I may be seen as a bit strange. So I waited for an opportunity.

Then the pastor asked the young lady what she did for a living.

Another woman – it turned out to be her mum – said, 'It's no use asking her. She doesn't do anything. She's been in a car accident. She's been having physio for two years now.'

There was my opportunity.

'Yes,' I said. 'Tell me about your shoulder and your left arm.'

'Uh? How did you know that was the problem?'

'Don't worry about that. That's just Jesus. He's here, you know. The thing is that when I looked at you, God showed me a picture of your left shoulder and your arm and you've got some injury there.'

'Yeah, but how do you know that?'

'I didn't really know, actually, but Jesus knew about it – and He loves you. He wants to heal you. Would you mind if I pray for you?'

'Yeah, I'd like that.'

'Great. You don't have to stand up. I'll come to you. Do you mind if I put my arm here and pray for the damaged shoulder?'

'Nah. Not at all.'

I placed my hand on her shoulder and silently prayed.

'The Spirit of God is on you, isn't He? And now – in the name of Jesus… I am just waiting on Him now.'

Suddenly I could sense the Spirit of God.

'Do you feel that?'

'Yeah, it's all getting hot.'

'That's good. Hot is good. That is the Holy Spirit; He's healing you there. Just receive that. In Jesus' name be healed right now.'

I took my hand off and asked her to stretch her arm out.

'Hey! It's better! Mum, look at this!'

'Jesus has healed you. That's fantastic. But you know what, He wants to do a greater miracle than that, right now. He wants to forgive your sins, and change your life. Jesus wants to come into your heart; you can be a brand-new person, you know. That's why He died for you. He paid the price for you. He's alive; He's risen. If you will receive Him now, He will forgive everything and make you new. Come on, why don't you give your life to Jesus?'

Suddenly the ladies said together, 'We'd all like that.' They all gave their lives to Jesus. Just like the woman at the well, these ladies were needy. They saw that it was better to believe than it was to argue.

And as for the pastor who didn't believe in the baptism of the Holy Spirit – well, let's just say, he had a rethink!

The word of wisdom

We've looked at something of the word of knowledge in operation. But what about the word of wisdom? Broadly these gifts work together but in the operation of the word of wisdom, this provides 'keys' so we know how to apply the word of knowledge, how to respond to a difficult question or situation, or to unlock relational conflict or doors that appear closed to some furtherance of His kingdom. It operates in times of ministry in church gatherings but also outside of active prayer and ministry. It operates very often in conversation.

I may be in a board meeting with my trustees and suddenly one of the trustees says something that opens up the whole conversation and leads us quickly to the right conclusions. That can be the word of wisdom in operation. Sometimes it operates through Christian businesspeople, politicians, or in family situations. I also have it operate a lot in evangelism where someone is just argumentative or resistant to the gospel. Many times the Lord gives a word that diffuses the situation or argument and just opens their heart to Jesus.

One time while ministering the gospel to a whole school, a Seventh-day Adventist school in Rwanda, I finished my presentation and gave the appeal, expecting students to respond for salvation. But no one responded! Not one! That was completely unexpected and a total shock for an evangelist who is used to seeing people respond. I opened up for questions, and quickly realised that these students were incredibly well versed in Scripture as they fired some of the deepest theological questions at me that I had ever encountered. They clearly did not believe that they could enter heaven without a fastidious observance of the Sabbath.

I did my best to present Christ as the fulfilment of the Law, taking them through the Law and the Prophets, on to the Gospels and Paul's letters that speak into the subject, but nothing would move them to change their position. A realisation suddenly dawned on me that I was dealing with a spiritual stronghold, and as I paused, the Holy Spirit suddenly reminded me of something Jesus said, so I repeated His words, stating, 'We must remember what Jesus said, "The Sabbath was made for man, not man for the Sabbath."'[162]

At that moment, the presence of God powerfully manifested in that school hall, there was a holy silence that came over everyone, and the headmaster stood up, declaring, 'I have seen something today that I never saw before. Christ is enough! I believe, and want to be baptised. Who will join me in giving their lives to Jesus today?'

The whole school raised their hands, and prayed with me, receiving the precious gift of salvation through Jesus Christ. Praise God! *That* was a word of wisdom opening the door for the gospel in the lives of those precious students and staff in Rwanda.

When to speak

We need wisdom along with the knowledge God gives to know when to speak; how to impart what God is giving us. Jesus knew what was in people's hearts,[163] but that doesn't mean He acted on every single thing He saw. He did what He saw the Father doing.[164] God's wisdom may sometimes be to do nothing with the knowledge that has been given at that present time. He has a way of revealing His purposes in the right way and at the right moment.

My good friend Gerald Coates tells of a time when God revealed to him a word and a strategy for the Prime Minister of the UK.[165] But as he didn't know the man, he reasoned God would bring about a way of speaking to him at a later date. What he didn't want to do was just send off some kind of letter or email that might be interpreted as Gerald being a bit of a nutcase! Sure enough, a day came soon after where he met the perfect person who was able to convey the message to the Prime Minister in a way that sounded reasonable. And sure enough, it was then acted upon in an appropriate way.

Sometimes, though, we are too hesitant. Notice Scripture calls it a 'word' of knowledge, and a 'word' of wisdom, not a 'paragraph' of knowledge or wisdom! Don't wait until you have the whole thing formed in your mind. We need to step out in faith with what God has given us and we will find that God gives us more. These gifts are so powerful for opening up closed situations and bringing about significant impact for the kingdom of God.

In closing, let me share with you a personal account of moving in the word of knowledge in evangelism, where the Holy Spirit so often releases these gifts to open up hearts and lives to the good news of Jesus. I was working with some churches in Derbyshire where they had bought a bus and were using it to reach out to the youth in the town. The night I arrived they were using it alongside a free barbecue with soft drinks for the kids on a local recreation ground. I asked the Lord to 'open a door of grace' for me to share the gospel, and within five minutes the gentleman cooking the burgers said to me, 'Last time you came up this way, Jon, I was an atheist, but you picked me out in a crowd saying that God wanted to heal me of asthma. I had had serious problems for years, but was instantly healed that night and gave my life to Christ!' His testimony became my door of opportunity as I called to the kids to gather round and hear this guy's story. As he spoke, it gave me a few minutes to 'look' into the crowd and 'see' what God was doing. He gave me a word of knowledge for one of the girls – that she had a problem with her neck and spine. I 'saw' it like an X-ray. It turned out it was a congenital condition.

Once the burger man's testimony was over, I called the youth to gather round and witness what God was about to do for this young lady. As we prayed, her neck and back suddenly visibly straightened and she was completely healed. There was no problem in preaching the gospel after that! I simply presented Jesus to them in a five-minute preach and gave an appeal… within moments forty-six of the girl's friends came to know Christ as Lord and Saviour, and a further thirty as the evening went on. The harvest is ripe and we are called to reap it![166] Let's go with confidence, asking the Lord to 'open our eyes' to see what He is doing, and then step out on the words, impressions, and visions He gives us. God does great things through small acts of obedience.

Endnotes

152. Acts 2:16-17 (ESV)
153. 1 Corinthians 2:9-10a (NIV)
154. 2 Timothy 3:16
155. John 5:19,30
156. Ephesians 1:20-22
157. Ephesians 1:3
158. Hebrews 5:11-14
159. Matthew 7:8
160. 1 Corinthians 6:18
161. John 4:1-42
162. Mark 2:27 (NIV)
163. Mark 2:8
164. John 5:19,30
165. Ralph Turner, *Gerald Coates: Pioneer* (Milton Keynes: Malcolm Down Publishing, 2015), pp178-179
166. Matthew 9:37-38

Chapter Eight:
The Revelation Gifts:
Discerning of Spirits

We live in a spiritual world. There is the kingdom of God and the domain or power of Satan. There are angels and demons. And of course, men and women are in essence spirit, though we live in a body.[167]

God has 'wired' some people to be particularly sensitive in the area of revelation, an area which includes, among other things, discerning of spirits. Often they are people with a prophetic call upon their lives.

God's wiring

It's God who wires us. It's God who gifts us. The psalmist says that He has knitted us together, even while we were in our mother's womb.[168] God knew us intimately before we ever knew Him.[169] He planned our days[170] – and He grants us His gifts.

Consequently, some of us may be more gifted than others in certain areas. We all have access to all the gifts of the Spirit, but it may be God has wired some of us more than others in certain areas of ministry.

I find this particularly in the prophetic and in the use of the word of wisdom and knowledge. Even before they become a Christian, some people don't know why, but they know things. And they don't know why they know these things. They feel things and they feel atmospheres. They are very sensitive. I call this 'prophetic personality'. It's to do with calling and destiny. Furthermore, I often find that Satan has recognised this calling on them, having been in heaven once, and has tried to get in first by offering them the occult, spiritualism and New Age. If they don't find Christ, the enemy will often find them and use them in the occult. Fundamentally, that's what's happening with fortune tellers that seem unwaveringly accurate. A good example would be the sorceress that speaks to Saul in the Old Testament.[171] It's the enemy's counterfeit of a genuine God-gift.

However, when people like this become Christians, and get delivered from their past and receive the baptism in the Holy Spirit, they take off quickly in the gifts of the Spirit, feeling God showing them things, moving sensitively with the Spirit of God, and they sense what is operating in a person or place.

It's great to see such believers learn to move with the Holy Spirit so quickly, but there is also a great need to teach them how to live by the Word of God too, and keep the Word as the final authority in every area of life and spiritual experience, otherwise they can be knocked about by everything they 'pick up' in the spirit in each situation they encounter. All believers, at every stage of their Christian walk, need to learn both sensitivity to the Holy Spirit and the stability of a walk of faith in the Word of God. To see such young believers move so freely in the Spirit may be frustrating at times for some believers who have walked faithfully with the Lord for years but have not continued to cooperate with the Holy Spirit in His gifts. But if we can allow this to provoke us, to stir up the gifts of God ourselves and at the same time lovingly disciple younger believers into being strong in the Spirit *and* the Word, it will be hugely beneficial to moving the whole body of Christ forward as mature sons and daughters of God, growing in discipleship and reaching our world for Christ.

Spiritual senses

The writer to the Hebrews says this:

> Though by this time you ought to be teachers, you have need again for someone to teach you the elementary principles of the oracles ['sayings'] of God, and you have come to need milk and not solid food. For everyone who partakes *only* of milk is not accustomed to the word of righteousness, for he is an infant. But solid food is for the mature, who because of practice have their senses trained to discern good and evil.[172]

The context of these verses is encouragement to grow up. How do we grow? By eating solid, healthy food, regular exercise and proper rest. This is also true in our Christian lives. A healthy diet of God's Word, a lifestyle of obedience, and a walk of faith-rest in the finished work of Christ brings about fast and strong development. And what is the result of this healthy kingdom lifestyle? It's being so in tune with God's Spirit and purposes that we can train our senses to discern good and evil.

Many in the Church today live in a perpetual state of spiritual babyhood. They are constantly on a 'sin, confess sin, sin, confess sin' cycle. But actually God intends, as new church pioneer Arthur Wallis once said, for the confession of sins to be the emergency exit rather than the daily staircase. Without understanding and embracing their identity in Christ and His finished work on their behalf – what Paul calls 'the gift of righteousness', and 'the abundance of grace', many believers haven't grown up and consequentially do not 'reign in life'.[173] For many, the trouble is that some of the ways in which we teach grace keeps people in this spiritual babyhood. They think of grace merely as a spiritual position, as only an *imputation* rather than also being an *impartation* of Christ's character and charisma. But let's embrace the reality that grace is not only about pardon, wonderful as that is, but also about power! Empowerment to become like Christ in every way. We have been called into a life-changing relationship with a heavenly Father who loves us, a Saviour who laid down His life for us, and His Spirit who transforms us into the fully mature sons and daughters of God He has called us to be, reflecting the glory and love of Christ in this world.

We are empowered by the Holy Spirit. We can train our senses to discern spirits; to discern good and evil. Let's settle this issue of righteousness. God has accepted us. As the writer to the Hebrews says, let's move onto solid food.

Discerning

God will help us to be discerning. He will help us to understand the spiritual atmosphere, and to know what to do. I was in an open-air meeting in Uganda. The Holy Spirit came upon us in a very gentle but powerful way. It was a beautiful time. Hundreds of people were getting baptised in the Holy Spirit all over the site. They were just lifting up their voices and finding that God met them with the gift of a beautiful new language.

Then, suddenly, things seemed to change. There was a sudden shout; then another. People began screaming and shouting across the site. It felt like war had broken out! Whole groups of people were falling to the floor. Others started to scream and writhe around like snakes.

It wasn't very hard for me to discern that something had happened! I sensed God telling me to get off the stage and go into the crowd. As I walked forward, wherever I went, anyone within about ten feet of me fell to the ground, some literally being thrown over the seats. Many who had clearly been gripped by an evil spirit were set free as I walked towards them, commanding the demons to leave in Jesus' name.

I could have missed it. I could have stayed on the stage wondering where the gentle atmosphere had gone. But with God's help, I was able not just to identify the change in the meeting, but to know what to do. We have a God who is both a gentle Shepherd and an immensely powerful 'Man of War'![174] And we must move with Him when the atmosphere changes and He starts to move in different ways. It's something we learn; a process over time and experience. David took on the lion and the bear in the privacy of the wilderness before he took on Goliath in full view of Israel's troops and her enemies.[175] The lessons he learned in the secret place became the keys to breakthrough in the public place. Private encounters precede public glory.

Don't get knocked about

In that meeting in Uganda, it would also have been very easy to get knocked about by the enemy. The spiritual atmosphere was intense. We need to be secure in Christ, and to inwardly *know* that we are secure, with complete authority over the enemy.

It's too easy for someone starting out in this area to be strong in the discerning of spirits, but to be weak in an understanding of our position in Christ. I have seen too many people get affected by what they are discerning. Someone may correctly discern, for example, that there is a strong evil presence in a place due, say, to the activities of a local witch's coven. They can be affected by it – almost frightened by it. But the truth is, God is greater! There is no need to get freaked out by what we discern, however harmful the spirit we discern may appear to be.

Stay strong in the Word. Prepare yourself with Scripture. Remember the enemy is defeated. Speak in the name of Jesus, with His authority, and believe what God says as the final authority. Don't get knocked about!

All spirits

It's important to note that this gift is the discernment of spirits. That's *all* spirits. The Holy Spirit. Evil spirits. The sense of the spirit of a person.

Human beings are spirit, God is a Spirit. Angels are spirits. Demons are spirits. When God allows us to see into this realm, it is a realm of spirits. That shouldn't be strange to us. We are looking through God's eyes. By the power of the Holy Spirit we are able to see the world around us, which is much more than the physical.

That means when you shake someone by the hand, you can actually discern their spirit. You can pick up what condition they are in spiritually.

Conversely, someone can sense the Holy Spirit in you when you touch or shake hands. That's the spirit world – just as real at the physical world.

Many church buildings in the Western world today have fairly large auditoriums and other rooms. In the week some churches rent them out for 'secular' conferencing. Pastor friends of mine tell me that on a number of occasions, delegates come through the doors of the building and sense something more. For some, there is such an awareness of peace and God's presence that they feel they have to return for a church service at the weekend – and as a result their lives are changed forever. The start of that journey was their spiritual senses being woken by the Holy Spirit.

Dealing with spirits

When I was working with Don Double, I often led the worship for him. The schedule could be gruelling. On some of Don's 'Autumn Tours' we would be away for two to three weeks at a time, visiting up to thirty churches, holding evangelistic meetings.

One time, in an Anglican church, I had just finished leading the worship and sat down in one of the front pews. I was tired and glad of the rest while Don spoke. Suddenly, right in front of me, I saw a large, dark, cloaked figure. He was at least nine feet tall, wearing a black cape and right next to the old stone pulpit. At that stage in my life, I had never come across Freemasonry and had no real idea as to what it was. But that was the word that came to mind. So I rebuked the spirit of Freemasonry in the place, and the figure immediately disappeared.

I thought no more of it until we were leaving at the end of the meeting. As I walked past the pulpit, I saw a plaque on the wall by the side of it – exactly where the evil spirit had been standing. As I read the words, it announced that this part of the building had been sponsored by the Freemasons and the plaque bore the Freemason emblem.

God has given stewardship of the earth to humankind.[176] And so wherever humanity yields authority to the enemy, the enemy comes to inhabit.

In later years, I have regularly come across the spirit of Freemasonry. I have sometimes found it manifest in an inability of a couple to conceive. I have seen the spirit as a black snake curled around the potential umbilical cord of a baby and as we have declared God's power, the snake has had to go. Nine months later, the couple have a baby in their arms. I've seen it happen a number of times.

Seeing with God's eyes

There's an Old Testament story that tells of Elisha and his servant. One morning the servant wakes up to find that the city they are staying in is surrounded by the enemy. There are horses and chariots everywhere. Then Elisha asks God to open the eyes of the servant to see what Elisha could see. In front of the young man was an awesome array of God's power – 'hills full of horses and chariots of fire'.[177]

When we operate with the gift of the discerning of spirits, we are looking through God's eyes. We are seeing things in the spirit that are not visible to the human eye, but are just as real.

Angels

Elisha and his servant were looking upon angels. Angels are all around us. The Psalms declare it:

> Bless the LORD, O you his angels,
> you mighty ones who do his word,
> obeying the voice of his word!
> Bless the LORD, all his hosts,
> his ministers, who do his will![178]

Angels respond to the word of the Lord. They respond to God's direction. And we have a God who answers our prayers. Without us knowing, God may often be answering our prayers through the activity of angels. Who knows how often God has protected us from harm by stationing angels around us? We don't worship them,[179] but they are there to help us.

Speaking of angels, the writer to the Hebrews says:

> Are they not all ministering spirits sent out to serve for the sake of those who are to inherit salvation?[180]

Angels are there to support us. They are there for those of us that inherit salvation. Too often we forget God's mighty ones, present to help us!

My father used to run an estate agents' business. One branch in particular was doing so poorly it might have needed to close.

My dad had been reading the two passages above with regard to angels, so he decided to pray and ask God to send out angels to bring in business. Without any other way of advertising, that branch broke all records in one month. There were forty-three houses sold in that month and so many coming onto the market that my dad ran out of For Sale signs!

A friend of mine serves in a healing ministry in the church. In one particular meeting, he was preaching but had to stop. The reason was four rows back from the front. There, as sure as anything, my friend could see an angel. Clearly no one else could, so he tried to carry on preaching. In the end he gave up, though, and began to ask God what it was all about.

As he looked more closely at the angel, he saw he was carrying something. In his hands were two new kidneys. God pointed out to my friend the man directly in front of the angel.

'Excuse me, sir, but do you have a problem with your kidneys?'

'Well, yes. I'm due to go into hospital next week for my first dialysis.'

'Well, that's amazing. There's an angel standing right behind you and he has two new kidneys for you. In Jesus' name be healed – receive two new kidneys!'

As my friend prayed, he saw the angel lean over the man and place the kidneys inside him. The man slumped to the floor under the power of God. Later verification from the hospital confirmed that the man no longer required any treatment.

Jesus the example

As always, Jesus is our example. In the Gospel of Mark we read of Jesus perceiving with His spirit what was in someone's heart.[181] Working with the Holy Spirit, we can discern the spirits.

God has used me directly in this way on a number of occasions. One such time I was back at a church that had been mightily blessed by the Holy Spirit the year before, when I had come to do a mission which then turned into twelve months of 'outpouring meetings'. People had been falling over in the Spirit all over the place. The organist had been too full of the Holy Spirit to play, and had eventually slumped to the floor under the power of God, closely followed by the other musicians. I had looked forward to returning to this church, but as I sat there before getting up to preach, I was uneasy. I sensed in my spirit that something was very wrong.

As I looked to my left I saw a large man there. And I mean large! But as I looked, I felt anger rising up inside me. I was perceiving what was in the man's heart. I don't normally do this – and my counsel would be not to do it unless you are very sure! – but as I went up to preach, I went over to the man. Overcoming my own fear (after all, this was a big man who could have floored me with one punch!), I spoke to him.

I put my finger to his chest and said, 'Stop it! The Lord says, stop it! The Lord showed me that you have been going around the house groups in this church and you have been spreading all kinds of rumours about the pastor. And I see a picture of you with a pair of scales. You are weighing the pastor on the scales and you are telling people that you are weighing him up. And you have been going around saying these things. But the Lord actually says to you that He is weighing *you* up in His scales and He is giving *you* time to repent, and if you don't, He is going to judge you. So stop it.'

With that I went to the front and preached to a very subdued congregation. I have only done something like that twice in all my years of ministry, and you have to be very sure it is the Lord. But there was no doubt about it – I perceived what was in the man's heart.

It turns out that I had heard from God rightly. The man had been a leader in the church but had been put out of leadership for immorality. He had been away from the main meetings for some time, but had been visiting the various house groups, talking about the pastor and judging him. That meeting was the first time he had returned to the main meeting.

We have a God of revelation. Step through the door. Ask God to reveal to you in words of wisdom, words of knowledge and by the discerning of spirits, what He is doing in people's lives. Keep your relationship with the Lord as sweet as you can and expect that He will use you. God is training your senses!

Endnotes

167. 1 Thessalonians 5:23
168. Psalm 139:13
169. Psalm 139:1-4
170. Psalm 139:16
171. 1 Samuel 28:7
172. Hebrews 5:12-14 (NASB)
173. Romans 5:17 (NASB)
174. Exodus 15:3
175. See 1 Samuel 17
176. Psalm 115:16
177. 2 Kings 6:15-17 (NIV)
178. Psalm 103:20-21 (ESV)
179. Colossians 2:18; Revelation 22:8-9
180. Hebrews 1:14 (ESV)
181. Mark 2:8

Chapter Nine:
The Power Gifts:
Gift of Faith

We've been looking at each of the gifts in turn, grouped into three main types. We've considered the proclamation gifts (speaking in tongues, interpretation, prophecy) and the revelation gifts (words of knowledge and wisdom, discerning of spirits). Now we turn to the power gifts, considered so because they *do something*; something miraculous. These are considered to be the gift of faith, the gifts of healings and the working of miracles.

We will be looking specifically at the gift of faith in this chapter. But we need to be aware that faith is with us, in us, all the time. It's part of the package! The moment we prayed a prayer inviting Jesus into our lives, we were exercising faith, a faith that was given to us through the Word that we heard.[182]

We have been saved by faith – and we live by faith. The Hebrew phrase for 'live' – *chayah* – means not only 'to live', but to breathe, be animated, alive, be preserved, live in happiness, and recover health. This is real life. This is living by faith! The writer to the Hebrews even indicates that without faith we cannot please God.[183] We all have that saving faith – and also a measure of faith equal to our call.[184] Paul talks about our faith 'growing abundantly'.[185] This suggests we can develop our faith; we can feed and exercise our faith, and certainly if we want it to grow and produce results, we must.

Faith in the Word

When we read the Word, the Bible, we will find faith in abundance. When we meditate on God's Word, the Holy Spirit gets to work. He imparts faith to us. What we read of in the Bible is real. There are people there that have gone before us. They have made mistakes – but they have also exercised faith and seen God respond and break through seemingly impossible situations in miraculous ways. We can learn from them.

When we are reading or listening to God's Word, He is able to impart faith in a special way. Paul says that 'faith comes by hearing, and hearing by the word of God'.[186] If we hear the Word of God preached but get no faith from it, there are only two conclusions... either it was not God's Word we heard, or we simply didn't 'hear' it! We must give ourselves to sincerely listening to His Word so that we really obtain faith through it. As a general rule, input equals output: little word, little faith, much word, much faith. Since both Jesus and Paul said that it was faith that releases the 'river' or 'supply' of the Holy Spirit, causing God to work miracles among us and through us,[187] it is clear that taking time to build our faith through reading, meditating and confessing the Word of God is foundational to a life of miracles.

Near the end of John's Gospel, John writes that

these [things] are written so that you may believe that Jesus is the Christ, the Son of God, and that by believing you may have life in his name.[186]

There it is again. We read what is written. It causes faith to arise so we believe. The result is life! Life in His name. The New Living Translation puts it as 'life by the *power* of his name'.[189] Faith promotes God's power and God's working in our lives. Time connecting with Him in the Word always results in faith.

The gift of faith

There is a faith that goes beyond the types of faith we have been discussing, and that is the gift of faith as expressed by Paul in his first letter to the Corinthians, chapter 12, verse 9. Some commentators refer to it as a 'special faith'.[190] It is a specific gift for a specific situation that goes well beyond our normal faith levels. It is a portion of God's unlimited faith for that situation at that moment.

And remember what we have already discussed – all the gifts are available to all believers!

On one occasion, while ministering as part of an evangelistic tent mission in Surrey, I came back from street work into an afternoon meeting that had been especially put on for the chronically sick. As I walked into the tent, I saw five wheelchairs lined up on the front row. Suddenly I felt an empowering from God. It was electric, like being connected up to the National Grid! I sensed a special anointing of the Holy Spirit, and perfect faith, special faith was in operation. I hadn't reached out for it, it just 'fell' on me, and I went with the obvious direction this was taking me.

I walked straight up to the first person in the wheelchair.

'Madam, would you like to walk?'

'Yes, please!'

'Then in Jesus' name, get up and walk!'

I took her by the hand, helping her up – and she walked, pushing her own wheelchair out of the tent.

My interaction with this first lady got the attention of the others in wheelchairs. I went along the line in turn, praying for them and commanding them to walk in Jesus' name.

The second one got up and walked. So did the third. So did the fourth.

When I asked the fifth person whether she wanted to walk, the response was slightly different: 'No, thank you, I'd lose my disability benefit!'

Well, God bless her. For her that evening, she was simply not ready to face life without a wheelchair. But for the other four, a new physical life began that night. Interestingly, the moment the lady in the fifth wheelchair said 'no, thank you', the anointing lifted off me. It was a gift to be received, but God doesn't force Himself on anyone. However, I didn't leave it there. I explained to the lady what had happened, in a non-condemnatory way, and then asked her if she would find a gradual recovery easier to handle. She said, 'Yes, it would give me time to adjust to a new way of living.' So we agreed that I would lay hands on her believing with her for a recovery, as Jesus promised in Mark's Gospel,[191] and that she would daily thank the Lord by faith for her healing and do a little more each day than she could do the day before. I felt nothing when I laid hands on her, but did so in faith for recovery. I met that lady two years later in a meeting in Croydon, near London, completely healed by the power of God! She told me that thirteen weeks later, while sitting in her lounge at home, after thanking God and acting in faith every day, the power of God, that same power she had felt in the tent meeting all those weeks back, suddenly fell on her and lifted her out of her wheelchair. She has never been in it since. Such interesting and wonderful lessons in the life of faith!

What I witnessed so sensationally that night was an imparting of the gift of faith, as described by Paul in 1Corinthians:

to another, faith by the same Spirit ...[192]

It's important to say that I'm the same as you. In other words, this isn't a special anointing for the 'man of power for the hour', but an anointing of faith that we can all experience.

Remember, the gifts of the Holy Spirit are available for all of us. Just as we can step out in faith and speak in tongues, so we can step out in the faith that we have, and when we reach the borders of our own faith levels, see God release His faith to take us further into His realm, the realm of the miraculous. It doesn't always start with a feeling, but it always starts with an obedient response to the Word of God, to the commission of Jesus: 'Heal the sick, raise the dead … cast out demons.'[193] Sometimes the revelation comes first and we step out, seeing what the Father is doing; other times we simply act on the written Word, the commission passed down to us from Jesus through His first apostles. Either way, He is faithful to fulfil His promises, and genuine, activated faith releases the manifestation of the Holy Spirit. It is a power partnership!

God never doubts

The portion of faith given me that night was from God, of course. It's not something I worked up. But at the same time, we need to be aware that we are much better prepared to receive the gift of faith when we are sowing to the Spirit on a regular basis through investing the promises of God like seed in the soil of our hearts. Inevitably, we will reap a harvest of miracles, gifts of the Spirit, and an overcoming and fruitful life in the kingdom if we embrace a life prepared for God.

God never has a bad day! There's never a day when God says, 'Well, I've been working hard in those revival meetings. I need a rest. I don't think I'll respond to any faith requests today.' No! God is not like that! He is the *same* 'yesterday and today and for ever'.[194] He is always there, always ready to respond. Always ready to give. Always ready to surprise us!

I read an article a while back where a preacher was saying that doubt is part of faith. Not at all! No way! The apostle Paul says in his letter to Rome, 'whatever is not from faith is sin.'[195] God wants us to live 'by faith, not by sight'.[196] We can overcome our doubts in the same way as we overcome unbelief, through turning from them to God, surrendering our mind to the transforming power of His Word that in turn changes our character and releases us into the experience of His amazing will for our lives.[197] Ultimately, faith is a choice; a choice to believe what God has said above what human beings, circumstances or feelings say. It is trusting in God's character, and His covenant with us. The integrity of God and blood of Jesus, His Son, stand behind every promise the Father ever made. We can choose to live by the tree of the knowledge of good and evil, which is the way of unbelief ('Has God said?'), or by the tree of life, Jesus Christ Himself, and what He has revealed to be the truth ('God has said!'). Choose faith, choose life.

Cultivating faith

There is a supernatural and sovereign element to God giving us the gift of faith as described in 1 Corinthians. However, there is much we can do to cultivate faith. The more we cultivate it and the more we exercise it, the greater the possibility that God will use us in miraculous ways with the gift of faith. I want to create every possibility for God to use me. How about you?

We can cultivate faith by reading the Word – 'faith comes by hearing'.[198] We can cultivate faith by remembering God's past faithfulness. As we look back with thankfulness, so faith grows for the future. We can cultivate faith by developing our knowledge of God. You cannot trust someone you don't know. If we get to know someone, we develop a relationship with them. As we pray and spend time in God's presence, it's easier for us to receive, just as we give to Him in our prayer and praise.

Faith is reinforced further through life's experiences, as we prove God's faithfulness.[199] Through our daily lives we can live and act in total dependence on God. Our dependence on faith in God meets with God's own faithfulness towards us. Faith becomes a relationship of trust, based on God's nature and promises towards us.

The more we have faith towards God, the more we experience His faithfulness and so our own faith grows. Fear is banished. We step out in faith and God meets us. In such fertile soil, God is able to bless and the gift of faith is exercised.

Not only does our faith grow as we consider God's faithfulness to us throughout life and ministry, but through our testimony to His faithfulness, faith is imparted to others also, which releases the power of God to be manifest in their lives too! One of our team members in Mission24, who is now a trustee of our ministry, started travelling with me alongside his father when he was just twelve years old. On one occasion, we went as a team to lead a large evangelistic mission in India, where tens of thousands responded to the call of salvation, and miraculous healings almost became commonplace as the gospel was proclaimed on the streets and in the evening events. On the closing Sunday I sent the team out to preach in the churches, and young Stephen went to preach at a village church. Following his message on the healing of the man with leprosy in Matthew chapter 8, an old Hindu grandmother walked slowly to the front dragging something behind her in a rough cotton bag.

'Does your Jesus still heal leprosy, young man?' she asked.

'Jesus can do anything!' Stephen responded.

At that point, the old lady reached back to her bag and opened it up to reveal a young girl of just seven years, with her flesh torn and scarred from leprosy. At that point, Stephen says that if faith was a feeling, he felt it drain out of him. However, he suddenly remembered the testimony I had once shared with him of a similar occasion when I had prayed for someone with leprosy in Ghana and seen him healed. Stephen proceeded to do exactly what I had done a number of years before. With the enemy screaming in his ear, 'Don't touch her or you'll become leprous too!' he reached out, taking hold of her arm, and prayed his best prayer of faith. Somewhere in the middle of that prayer, the gift of special faith was released, Stephen 'knew' the work was done, and as he opened his eyes, he witnessed a weeping grandmother taking off all the clothes of her young granddaughter to check her whole body, because the leprosy had instantly disappeared and the child was made whole. This is the power of testimony; one miracle giving birth to another. Let us grow strong in our faith. Faith in the faithfulness of God.

God empowerment

For all of us, there can be times when we sense God coming close to us. It may feel like God dropping down onto us – almost a sense of God's weight on us. It may feel like God has wrapped a cloak around us. We may sense physical warmth and power or simply an awareness that God is doing something amazing. That's the gift of faith. Let's ask God for it, believe we receive it, and step out in faith expecting it. It's a transforming and powerful gift of the Spirit.

Word and Spirit

Many churches may claim to operate as churches that follow the Spirit's leading. Others may say that they are wholly dependent on the Word. And it can be the same for each of us as individual believers.

One may say, 'Well, I'm totally reliant on the Holy Spirit. I won't do anything He doesn't say.'

Another may say, 'I soak myself in the Word of God. It's the Bible I look to for my strength and direction.'

Which is right? The Spirit or the Word? The answer is – both! We are not to be entirely a 'Spirit people' or entirely a 'Word-directed people'. We are to be entirely both.

The story is told of David Morgan during the 1859 revivals in Wales. Morgan had been praying for revival for over ten years. He was serious about God moving. One night he awoke and felt a strange anointing. He was conscious that at that moment a mysterious change had come over him. He became aware that he was suddenly able to remember every single thing he had been taught as a Christian. He was able to recite any passage from God's Word. He could recall every sermon ever preached to him.

With this anointing, God empowered him in the revival meetings in a supernatural way. He was able to remember anything and everything that was said to him during a meeting – names, dates of birth, spiritual and physical conditions, family needs, everything. This supernatural imparting from God was used to great effect.

The anointing lasted for around two years. Then one night, as Morgan slept, it was gone, and he woke the next day with just the usual ability to remember.[200]

Such an anointing speaks of how the Holy Spirit brings back to our remembrance things that Jesus has said and, indeed, whatever we need to know at a given moment. It's also an incredible and specific faith impartation, which Morgan was able to use in the revival meetings to see many saved and healed.

He had been praying for revival for ten years. There had been a long period of preparation; a long time in the Word. Then the Spirit came. When the Spirit came, He illuminated the Word! It was the Bible that Morgan was able to remember, along with every godly sermon he'd ever heard.

May I encourage you, as we finish this chapter, to be a 'both/and' person, not an 'either/or' person! Let's get deep into His

Word. We can expect that faith will rise as we study the Word; that's what the Word promises.[201] And let's be expectant for mighty and powerful moves of the Holy Spirit as special anointings of the gift of faith are imparted. After all, that's also what the Word promises.[202] Let's step out in faith and expect it!

Endnotes

182. Romans 10:17
183. Hebrews 11:1,6
184. Romans 12:3
185. 2 Thessalonians 1:3 (ESV)
186. Romans 10:17 (NKJV)
187. John 7:37-39; Galatians 3:1-6 (ESV)
188. John 20:31 (ESV)
189. Author italics
190. D. Guthrie et al (editors), *New Bible Commentary* (Leicester: IVP, 1970), p1067
191. Mark 16:18
192. 1 Corinthians 12:9 (ESV)
193. Matthew 10:8 (ESV)
194. Hebrews 13:8 (NIV)
195. Romans 14:23 (NKJV)
196. 2 Corinthians 5:7 (NIV)
197. Romans 12:1-2
198. Romans 10:17 (NKJV)
199. Hebrews 11:6
200. You can read more in Eifion Evans, *Revival Comes to Wales* (Bridgend: Evangelical Press of Wales, 1979), pp53-54
201. Romans 10:17
202. 1 Corinthians 12:11

Chapter Ten:
The Power Gifts:
Gifts of Healings

Healing is in the nature of God.[203] Healing is in the character of God, a central part of who He is and His desire for us to be whole. When we look at the ministry of Jesus, the Word made flesh, the embodiment of the Father's will, He never made anyone sick, and never refused to heal anyone who came to Him for healing or deliverance. It's so important in this area, as in any other, that our faith lines up with what Scripture reveals as the will of God, because true faith begins where the will of God is known and acted upon.

The fullness of Christ's sacrifice encompassed healing. God knew before the beginning of time that He would sacrifice His Son on our behalf. His sacrifice was so certain that the book of Revelation calls Jesus 'the Lamb slain from the foundation of the world'.[204] And as Christ died on the cross, sin's authority was forever broken and Satan has no more legal claim on anyone who names Jesus Christ as their Saviour and Lord. Salvation has come. And so has healing.[205] Of course, Jesus healed before the cross, and forgave sins too. But His sacrifice was an eternal sacrifice reaching all the way back to Adam's sin, and all the way forward to the end of the age. Forgiveness of sins and healing for soul and body have been provided through the finished work of Jesus to all who call on His name.

Just as we are saved and are still being saved day by day until the final day, so with healing. Our bodies are not yet fully redeemed in the sense of our perfect resurrection bodies until the day Christ returns. But at the same time, we can live in gratitude for what Jesus has accomplished through the cross on our behalf. We can appropriate the health that God has for us in Christ on a daily basis. If we are sick or in pain we can reach out in faith to our heavenly Father and expect healing, whether that comes through taking communion, receiving laying on of hands, anointing with oil by the elders, or just standing in faith on His finished work and declaring our healing with faith and praise. That's the wonder of Christ's death on the cross. He died for our sins – 'he was pierced for our transgressions … by his wounds we are healed'.[206]

In the Old Testament, straight after their deliverance from Egypt, the Lord spoke to Israel, saying these words:

If you will diligently listen to the voice of the LORD your God, and do that which is right in his eyes, and give ear to his commandments and keep all his statutes, I will put none of the diseases on you that I put on the Egyptians, for I am the LORD, your healer.[207]

God has made a covenant to heal. It's not just an intention, it's a promise. We can step out on the firm promises of God and expect healing.

Death is not a friend

Jesus came to give us life, and 'life in all its fullness'.[208] He did not come to give us sickness, pain or death. Death is not a friend. Death is not ultimate healing. Death is an enemy of God that will finally be destroyed at the coming of the King! Dying and going to heaven is not healing; that's an important reality. Even in the Old Testament the Lord said, 'choose life, that you … may live'.[209] The order is significant. The experience follows the decision, and the fact that our God has revealed Himself to be our Healer means that we can look to Him in faith. We can choose life, thank God!

Death in this age is as a result of Adam's fall. It will be reversed when Christ returns. In the meantime, how do we live? By not accepting death in our lives on a daily basis! By not accepting sickness. By being aware that God's intention and provision for us is for full health and to stand in that.

It's good to continue to contend for healing no matter how ill a person may be. I work occasionally with a lady on our Mission24 team who was miraculously healed from cancer when her prognosis was that she had just a few months to live. If my friend Linda had not allowed someone to pray for her, by 'accepting death' – by accepting the doctor's diagnosis – she would not have been healed.[210]

Healing is only for this age, of course, not for the age to come. In that future age there will be no sickness or disease. But for today, there may be times in any believer's life when we may need healing. And we can call on God for that healing. He wants to heal, and we should expect that He will.

A good friend of ours was struck down with sepsis, a killer infection. By God's grace he pulled through and is now in recovery. When he was asked what his long-term prognosis was, he announced, 'God's prognosis is full health!' I love that statement of faith. It's totally in line with God's intentions for us.

No condemnation

God's intention is good health. But what happens if we do not appear to be healed? Sometimes healing is a gradual thing, so don't give up! And don't be condemned either. Paul tells us there is no condemnation in Christ.[211] Healing is very much a grace thing. The Gospel of Mark tells us the sick will recover.[212] It appears to be written in the context of a gradual recovery.

If we do not appear to receive healing, let's not get condemned about it or beat ourselves up for a supposed lack of faith. Let's continue to thank God and trust that healing will come. No condemnation. But no giving up either! Jesus' teaching on faith encourages us to believe that we *have* received something that we ask for in prayer, *before* we can see or feel it.[213] That should be expressed in our words, acknowledging His faithfulness, and praising Him for the answer *before* we yet experience it. God inhabits such praise and releases miracles in our lives that way.

I remember ministering in a United Reformed Church on the Isle of Wight. At the end of the meeting, during a time of ministry, a man in his fifties came up to me explaining that his hearing was so bad the doctors had given him just three months before he would be entirely deaf. With an expression of great determination on his face, he held his hearing aids out to me in his hands, and said, 'I have had enough of these!' I liked his attitude, and encouraged him to believe God while I laid hands on him for healing.

By the grace of God, we have seen many people healed of various measures of deafness through the years, but on this occasion, following prayer, it appeared that he was no better. There were many queuing up for prayer that night, so I suggested he get on his knees and worship the Lord, and said that when the presence of God increased upon him, I would return and pray for him again. After praying for many people that night, forty minutes later, to be exact, I looked around to see this dear gentleman utterly lost in worship, with tears running down his cheeks, and the presence of God tangibly over him. I knelt in front of him, and with my hands on his ears simply commanded them, 'Be opened, in Jesus' name'. Within moments he burst out in praise testifying that he could hear, and perfectly at that. It was such a joy to receive a personal letter from his wife three months later, testifying that her husband's ear specialists had medically confirmed, with some degree of surprise, 100 per cent hearing had been restored. Jesus taught us 'always to pray, and not [to] lose heart'.[214] If there's one thing I've learned in this area of ministry, it's *don't give up!*

Praying for the sick

There are specialists in God's kingdom, for sure, those with a ministry in the gifts of healing.[215] That reflects the gifts of the Spirit, and the diversity of the body of Christ. Some may receive a particular gift anointing for healing. But, as with all the gifts of the Spirit, they are all available to us, and we need to reach out in faith expecting healing to flow as we minister to those in need of it.

One of the most common questions I get when teaching on healing is, 'What if I don't feel anything when I pray for someone?'

Often we will sense the power of the Holy Spirit at work, and I do encourage people to give some time for the Spirit to manifest when praying for people, which is often experienced as a heat in the hands, or in the affected area of the body of the one we are praying for. But that's not to be our basis for expectation. We pray for healing in obedience, and in line with the promises of God. He promises His best for the lives of the people we are praying for. The evangelist Reinhard Bonnke says, God is always at the zenith of His power.[216] We may not feel His presence, we may feel nothing has happened when we pray, but something always happens when we as believers in Christ pray. God is there. And He's always ready to move in power in and through our lives. Let's stay in faith and not withdraw our expectation because of feelings. Some of the greatest miracles I have ever experienced, including the raising of the dead, happened without me feeling a single thing.

My co-author Ralph Turner was once asked to pray for a man who had a severe back problem. Ralph says he was in a hurry. There was so much to do. He didn't feel he had the time to pray. He admits his attitude was not all it should have been. But he prayed – a short, perfunctory prayer, before rushing off to do something else. Imagine Ralph's amazement the next Sunday in church when the same man came over to him to thank him for the prayer. The moment Ralph had prayed, God had healed! It really is God who heals, not us.

Actually, God's power is made perfect in our weakness.[217] Paul spoke of a 'thorn … in the flesh'[218] but he kept on preaching. God's miracle-working power is made perfect in our inability to produce results.

Healing grace

In Matthew chapter 10, we read of Jesus sending out the disciples to 'Heal the sick, raise the dead, cleanse those who have leprosy, drive out demons. Freely you have received; freely give'.[219] Do you see what comes after the command to go? We have received freely. That means we can give freely. It's not dependent on our maturity. We don't have to work up some kind of faith or wait until we feel a special anointing. It's great if that happens, but don't wait for it. Step out. Give freely. It's God who heals. We have healing grace!

We have similar instructions to these in the Great Commission of Matthew's Gospel:

And Jesus came and said to them, 'All authority in heaven and on earth has been given to me. Go therefore and make disciples of all nations, baptizing them in the name of the Father and of the Son and of the Holy Spirit, teaching them to observe all that I have commanded you.'[220]

Jesus not only commanded them to pray, to live holy lives, to love one another, but also to heal the sick, to cast out demons, raise the dead and preach the kingdom. His commands to them are commands to us.

Look at where the authority lies. It's with Jesus, not with us. Our authority is not inherent; our authority is delegated. The instructions in the Great Commission are for all of us. The Great Commission rolls down the ages, applying to each and every believer. And with those instructions comes the authority and grace to operate in them. Just as with the early disciples, we have that same delegated authority.

We are instructed to go, but not in our own authority: in the authority of the One who has conquered death, overcome the evil one, broken the chains of death and released healing through His own suffering. We have healing grace. Grace from God that's not in our strength, but in His. The power that broke death is the power in us,[221] delegated by God's grace.

Healing ways

Psalm 107 says that God sends His word to heal.[222] He sends healing. There are so many ways God can heal. It's good to be able to lay hands on people for their healing, but that's not always possible. I have led missions with upwards of 30,000 people. There's no way I or my team can pray for everyone personally or lay hands on them.

But the psalmist says God 'sends'[223] His word. I can 'send' that word from the microphone. God is more than able to heal in that way – or in any other way that His word reveals. God is directive in His healing power. I can direct God's words through the microphone. The Old Testament word for the Spirit of God is *ruach*. This means literally the 'breath that is released over the vocal organs when the word is spoken'. That's very specific and directional. The Holy Spirit brings to pass what the Word of God authorises – and with power. Let's learn to speak His words, to command with faith in the name of Jesus!

There are many healing methods, of course. The laying on of hands is one of the primary ways, when this is possible. This is reflective of its place as a foundational aspect of our faith. Hebrews chapter 6 records a number of what the writer calls 'elementary doctrines'.[224] The principle of laying hands on someone as we pray for them includes and goes beyond healing, and it is very effective. We are placing our hand on the person (often on the arm or shoulder – please be careful where you place your hands!) and, by God's grace, we are imparting healing to them. They may often sense a power or anointing as we do this. And so may we. We may feel a heat or something like electricity passing through our hands into the person we are praying for, for example. But it's not essential to sense the presence of God through our hands. God is more than able to heal without us feeling something first. There have been many occasions when God has surprised me by healing someone when I felt no Holy Spirit presence at all!

Speaking a word of command in faith is another method of praying for healing. I use this a lot when I am in front of big crowds, but we can all do this. We can speak with God's authority into a situation, and may combine this with the laying on of hands. We may well sense the authority which comes from God and we can speak that out, declaring healing. It may be appropriate to speak directly to the sickness or illness, especially where we feel that the enemy may be at work and there needs to be a release from the demonic. I also find that if there is a sense of resistance from something demonic, I may need to lead the person through some short prayers of confession and repentance from known sins, of forgiveness towards those who have hurt them or their loved ones in some way, renewing their faith in Jesus. Once these things are dealt with, there is normally little resistance left to deal with and once commanded to leave in Jesus' name, the demons go.

Elders anointing with oil in the name of the Lord is another method of praying for the sick, as directed in the book of James:

> Is anyone among you sick? Let him call for the elders of the church, and let them pray over him, anointing him with oil in the name of the Lord. And the prayer of faith will save the one who is sick, and the Lord will raise him up.[225]

Note it's the prayer of faith that heals the sick – not the prayer of hope! As elders or leaders, be bold in your prayers. Speak out the promises of Scripture and expect that God will move. Once again, we need to remember healing is by God's grace, but is to be ministered and received through faith.

Evangelism and the gift of healing

There is a specific gift of healing identified in Paul's first letter to the Corinthian church,[226] and there are also times when 'the power of the Lord [is] present to heal'[227] and a large number of people may get healed at one time in a meeting, whether it's an obviously Christian gathering, or in a more evangelistic situation. It's a special anointing from God. Someone may move in that gift on a regular basis, or they may have a special gift of healing anointing for a particular meeting or situation. Either way, when the Holy Spirit moves in power, He convicts, challenges and opens people's hearts to Jesus and their need of Him.

God has used me on occasion in this way. I may hear His prompting through the Holy Spirit, telling me in a meeting to start by praying, say, for damaged limbs, or for deaf ears. When God does that, I find most are instantly healed, whereas in general prayer I may find maybe half are healed, at least in terms of instantaneous healing. I don't make a doctrine out of it, but it's clear to me that when God directs specifically, there are often more healings as the gift of healing is in operation. I cannot ignore the fact that 99 per cent of the healing Jesus ministered into people's lives was instantaneous, and He did what He 'saw' the Father doing.[228] He is our model for ministry.

As we have already seen, there are instantaneous healings and there are recoveries. It is encouraging to know that if we don't get an instantaneous miracle, we can still recover! However, we should do our best to learn how to actively cooperate with the Holy Spirit so that we might represent Jesus as authentically as we can, and see more and more miracles that meet the needs of suffering humanity, lead people to a living faith in Jesus, and bring glory to God.

In Canada one time, the pastor I was working with in Ontario arranged an outside barbeque for forty or so people from a local housing estate, calling it a 'Healing Extravaganza'! Free burgers and cans of Coke were distributed, with an invite to experience the healing power of God. He told me I was not allowed to preach, but that he would introduce me and then I was just to get up and 'do the business'! Once introduced, I fairly casually said 'hi' to everyone, told them that God loved them and wanted to heal them of their suffering. I proceeded to ask the Lord where I should start. I felt I specifically heard the Spirit whisper to me to start with praying for joints that were damaged. There was this big guy there, walking with crutches. He slowly stepped forward, grimacing as he moved, clearly in lots of pain. I asked him what was wrong.

He said, 'I'm a construction worker. I fell from three floors up and landed on a spike. It broke my hip and my spine. I am full of wire. I have bolts in here and I live in constant pain.'

On the inside I was saying, 'Jesus, we could have started with a headache!'

As I prayed, I felt nothing. I was having an internal conversation with God and I began to pray under my breath in tongues, wanting to feel something. He had directed me to start with this man, but was not giving me any sense of His presence or power as I prayed. I was at least hoping to have hot hands – something God has given me before as an evidence of a healing anointing flowing – but there was nothing! I laid my hand on his shoulder and prayed in tongues.

Suddenly, I heard God tell me to stop making a big deal of it and tell the man to bend down. After hearing that several times, I did so.

'I can't do that.'

'I know, sir. I know that you have not been able to. But God is healing you. Bend down and see what happens.'

He began to bend. Suddenly he jerked upright again. His wife and young son were sitting near him, with an astonished look on their faces.

'I haven't been able to bend that far in twenty years!' he said.

'Well, don't stop now. Do it again, sir. Bend further.'

This time he bent all the way down and touched his toes. His face, which had been pretty much in the shape of a scowl, softened.

'I want to walk,' he said.

I encouraged him to throw his crutches to the ground and, leaning on me, he began to walk. Suddenly, you could feel the power of God tangibly fall on him, and he let go of me and started to run around the community hall where we were all sitting. His young son got up from his seat and jumped into the arms of his father.

'Daddy! Daddy! We can play football together now!'

His wife was sobbing by now. Everyone was in tears. As I briefly shared the gospel, every one of the people there gave their lives to Christ.

The gift of healing can be a powerful evangelistic tool, revealing the power and the compassion of Jesus to a hurting world.

God's medicine bottle

We can be healed through supernatural manifestations of the Holy Spirit, but we can also be healed through reading, inwardly digesting and confessing God's Word. There is power in the Word. It is, after all, the inspired Word of God, and has the ability to speak to us, to increase our faith and, through that process, to heal.

Bible teacher Derek Prince used to call a certain passage in Proverbs chapter 4, 'God's medicine bottle'.[229] Let's look at the text:

My son, be attentive to my words; incline your ear to my sayings. Let them not escape from your sight; keep them within your heart. For they are life to those who find them, and healing to all their flesh.[230]

That word 'healing' in this context in the Hebrew language can be translated as 'medicine to all their flesh'. Most medicine has to be taken two to three times a day to produce the expected cure. In the same way, we must immerse ourselves in the Word of God where healing is concerned, fixing our eyes on the promises, listening to them, meditating on them and speaking them out. There is real healing that can come that way; healing that comes through receiving the Word into our hearts and then confessing it through our mouths. Where we are seeking healing for ourselves, and that healing hasn't yet arrived, let's consider soaking ourselves in the Word of God. Allow the Word to fill us, challenge us and direct us. As we do so, God is more than able to apply the Word in faith, resulting in our healing.

Confessing God's healing with our mouth is so important. After all, that's the way we got saved! Dwell on scriptures that speak of healing and then speak them out. There is something faith-affirming when we speak God's promises out loud. But it's not just faith-affirming, it's salvation-releasing – *sozo* in the Greek used in the New Testament means salvation, but much more. It also means healing, deliverance, wholeness and protection!

Paul, writing to the Church in Rome, says that if we confess with our mouths that Jesus is Lord and believe in our heart that God raised Jesus from the dead, we will be saved.[231] We can extend that – we will be healed and delivered. The sense of the passage relates to the Greek legal system where a contract is signed. As we 'confess with our mouths', we are contracting with God. And where God signs up, things get done. On the other hand, there are some things relating to illness that we should never sign up to and definitely 'return to sender'!

Biblical testers

I'm aware as I write this that for many readers these will be new ideas. Too many have been brought up on a theology that allows for long-term sickness that works on the principle of prayers that say, 'If it be Thy will, God...' Well, it's always Gods will to heal! Here are three biblical 'testers' to help you:

1. Look at what the Bible shows us of life before sin came in, and what life is like after Christ's return. Without sin, the will of God is perfectly expressed. And that expression is without sickness.

2. Look at God's covenant names. One of them is Jehovah *Rophe* – the Lord your healer.[232] There is no doubt about God's intentions when one of his names is that He is a healing God.

3. Jesus never refused to heal anyone. Right through Scripture, anyone that asked Him was healed. He is the same, yesterday, today, and forever.[233] What confidence for you and I to pray in His name today!

The battleground of the mind

The Argentinian Christian leader Ed Silvoso argues that the spiritual battles in our lives are not so much in the heavenly places as between our ears![234] The enemy is spoken of as the 'prince of the power of the air',[235] but he attacks through our minds: that's where a lot of the battles take place. That's often where the strongholds are.

Paul declares that 'we are not ignorant of [the devil's] schemes'.[236] Another translation of the Greek word used for 'schemes' (*noema*) is 'mind' or 'mind games'.[237] We are not unaware of the mind games the devil plays. But we don't have to give in to those mind games!

A stronghold in the mind is a mindset that is impregnated with hopelessness, which causes us to accept as unchangeable the things that we know are contrary to the will of God. The devil's mind games mean we begin to think that things can't be changed, that healing will never happen. If we begin to make a theology for ourselves about why we believe that somebody wasn't healed, we have fallen for the devil's mind games.

Our theology must come from Christ and the Word of God, not from our personal experiences or failures. What would happen if Jesus were in any particular situation where healing was needed? He'd heal! That's the truth – Jesus would step up and heal as the request for healing was made. That has to be our active theology when we pray and minister.

It is sad to see some develop a theology that provides various excuses for lack of healing power. Some blame it on an earlier generational curse or words spoken over a person or place, but if that were true, surely Jesus would have attempted to break such curses off people? Or perhaps the apostles operated that way? The problem is that an honest look at the Gospels and book of Acts does not produce any examples of either Jesus or the apostles attempting to break generational curses off people or places in order to bring about greater freedom, healing or effectiveness in ministry.

At times, there may need to be some deeper ministry to ensure the person we are ministering to is able to receive God's forgiveness, has forgiven others or has repented of known sins – sometimes even leading to casting out demons – but we should not be looking for these issues as a first-off approach to healing ministry. The Holy Spirit will direct us, giving us words of knowledge and wisdom or discerning of spirits where we need it. Many are healed without needing to work through any repentance or forgiveness or needing any deliverance. Let us learn to stand on the promises of God and listen to the Holy Spirit when praying for those who are suffering. Jesus has the keys of their freedom, and His anointing can break any bondage.

Fasting for breakthrough

There are times when we may need to add fasting to our prayers if we are going to experience a breakthrough. We see this in the passage where Jesus tells the disciples that the epileptic boy will be healed only by prayer and fasting. Here are the verses:

When Jesus saw that the people came running together, He

rebuked the unclean spirit, saying to it: 'Deaf and dumb spirit, I command you, come out of him and enter him no more!' Then the spirit cried out, convulsed him greatly, and came out of him. And he became as one dead, so that many said, 'He is dead.' But Jesus took him by the hand and lifted him up, and he arose. And when He had come into the house, His disciples asked Him privately, 'Why could we not cast it out?' So He said to them, 'This kind can come out by nothing but prayer and fasting.'[238]

Many versions omit the 'fasting' bit as not being in the original – but other versions include it! What do we do with this text? The clue is in an earlier verse – verse 19:

'You unbelieving generation,' Jesus replied, 'how long shall I stay with you? How long shall I put up with you? Bring the boy to me.'[239]

The reason the boy was not healed by the disciples is because of their unbelief. One of the best ways to build belief is by prayer and fasting. Prayer and fasting doesn't change God – but it does change us!

Electricity comes into our house. It is a powerful current. But (thankfully in the context of our house!) the electricity is passed through a fuse board that regulates the level of the electricity by way of resistance and makes it safe and useable for a whole variety of applications. Good for a house. Not good for us in operating with the Holy Spirit. Let's ensure there is no 'resistance' between us and the Holy Spirit. Fasting and prayer reduces the resistance in our flesh to the work of the Holy Spirit in us and through us. And a lower resistance in this power partnership equals a higher flow of the power of God.

I had the privilege of meeting David Hogan.[240] David ministers in some of the hardest, most desperate parts of the world. He fasts every second day of his life. That's some commitment! But I have to say that the results speak for themselves – he has personally raised thirty-one people from the dead and seen many creative miracles.

I find fasting hard, but did spend a prolonged period of time fasting every other day a few years back. I can honestly say it was one of the most productive times in my ministry, especially in terms of seeing people healed of 'terminal' conditions, and casting out demons. In all honesty, I don't know anyone in the healing ministry who has had any sort of breakthrough anointing in this realm who hasn't given a significant time to fasting. It is not a requirement for healing in every situation, but may be necessary on those occasions where a greater breakthrough of Holy Spirit power is needed.

Contending for healing

There are times when God heals instantly. There are other times when we need to contend for healing, whether by prayer and fasting, or simply by holding on in faith that God will move. We have to fight for our health sometimes; we have to fight for our healing. We have to contend for our brothers and sisters. I have ministered to some people who have stood in faith for years for their healing, or for that of a loved one, until the moment came and they were completely restored to health. The enemy knows the reality of the healing power of God through the Church of Jesus Christ, and he knows how powerful the prayers of God's people are. Delay is not denial. Keep contending.

Robert Kayanja, a well-known pastor in Uganda, got angry with the spread of AIDS and HIV in his country. At one time it was estimated that one in every four adults had AIDS or HIV in the capital, Kampala. Robert held a mission in Kampala and declared war on AIDS. Within a few days, twenty people had been healed of AIDS/HIV. Other faiths objected to the mission and to the claims of healing. There was some violence and the army had to step in. The President of Uganda declared that the issue would be settled by sending all twenty off to the doctors to check the healing.

All twenty came back with a clean bill of health. That settled it. The army even helped with the security of the meetings after that! A further sixty people were healed of AIDS/HIV over the rest of the time of the mission, leading to many turning to the Lord for salvation.

In summary, healing is for today. In fact, it has to be for today, because there will be no need for healing in the new heavens and earth!

There's no one way someone is healed. But there is one thing for sure – God intends healing. Be in faith that God wants to heal and move out in faith as you pray for people.

Be persistent. Not all healing happens at once. Healing is in the Word of God, in the name of Jesus, and by the power of the Holy Spirit, but most of all by God's goodness, faithfulness and grace. If we remember that, we will see, by God's grace, many mighty healings.

Endnotes

203. Exodus 15:26
204. Revelation 13:8 (NKJV)
205. Isaiah 53:5
206. Isaiah 53:2-5 (NIV); see also 1 Peter 2:24; James 5:13-16
207. Exodus 15:26 (ESV)
208. John 10:10 (NCV)
209. Deuteronomy 30:19 (ESV)
210. You can read Linda's amazing story in: Ralph Turner, *Cheating Death, Living Life* (Maidstone: River Publishing, 2013)
211. Romans 8:1

212. Mark 16:18

213. Mark 11:24

214. Luke 18:1 (ESV)

215. 1 Corinthians 12:28

216. Christ for All Nations Bible Studies, https://www.cfan.org.uk/connect/bible-studies/fire-heaven (accessed 18.8.17)

217. 2 Corinthians 12:9

218. 2 Corinthians 12:7 (ESV)

219. Matthew 10:8 (NIV, US version)

220. Matthew 28:18-20a (ESV)

221. Romans 8:11

222. Psalm 107:20

223. (Amplified, Classic Edition)

224. See Hebrews 6:1-2 (ESV)

225. James 5:14-15a (ESV)

226. 1 Corinthians 12:9

227. Luke 5:17 (KJV)

228. John 5:19,30

229. Derek Prince, *God's Medicine Bottle* (New Kensington, PA: Whitaker House, 1984)

230. Proverbs 4:20-22 (ESV)

231. Romans 10:9

232. Exodus 15:26

233. Hebrews 13:8

234. Ed Silvoso, *That None Should Perish* (Ventura: Regal Books, 1994), p154

235. See Ephesians 2:2 (NKJV)

236. 2 Corinthians 2:11 (NASB)

237. Biblehub.com

238. Mark 9:25-29 (NKJV)

239. Mark 9:19 (NIV)

240. Leader of Freedom Ministries, a ministry to the indigenous people of Latin America

Chapter Eleven:
The Power Gifts:
Working of Miracles

There's a key difference between healing, as we've been looking at in the last chapter, and miracles, as we're going to be looking at in this chapter. Healing can be instant, and especially so when it is through a gift of healing, but it may also be gradual. Miracles, however, are always instantaneous and can also be creative.

The lame and the maimed

The Gospel of Matthew, chapter 15, says this:

> Then great multitudes came to Him, having with them the lame, blind, mute, maimed, and many others; and they laid them down at Jesus' feet, and He healed them. So the multitude marveled when they saw the mute speaking, the maimed made whole, the lame walking, and the blind seeing; and they glorified the God of Israel.[241]

We're looking at the New King James Version (NKJV) to make the point. It says it better than some translations. Among those brought to Jesus were the lame and the maimed. There's a difference, and not all the versions bring this out. The New Revised Standard Version (NRSV) says it too, as does Young's Literal Translation (YLT). Look carefully at the translations here – Young's aims to be as literal as possible to the original Greek.

167

Consequently, Young goes with describing the lame and the maimed, as do the NKJV and the NRSV. Many others simply refer to the lame and the crippled. As far as I can see, the three versions listed have the better translation.

Why go on about the different versions? Because lame people can still walk. They may be able to hold down a job. But the maimed have a more severe problem. If you are maimed, you lack a limb, or your limb is mutilated. You lack the ability to use that part of your body. It's mutilated or not there at all.

Jesus heals the lame *and* the maimed. The passage says the multitude marvelled when they saw the lame walking and 'the maimed made whole'. In other words, Jesus is creating new body parts. That's miraculous! An instantaneous creative act that produces missing limbs is amazing! This is more than healing, restoring to health something that is sick or diseased. This is miraculous, creative; a supernatural replacement of something lost.

By God's grace I have seen some of this in my ministry. I've seen at least a portion of a leg grow back, and in another scenario, new muscle and skin created. I've also seen metal rods inside a person disappear as the bone is renewed. This has later been confirmed in X-rays where the metal is simply not there.

A friend in ministry has seen the metal within the body that was holding the bones together literally dissolve, come out of the pores of the body and onto the floor, then solidify again as metal. The person was not hurt in the least when this happened.

A new inner ear

I was ministering in Canada and seeing a good number of significant healings. I felt prompted at one point in the meeting to pray for anyone that was deaf. God healed deaf ears that night, but one story stays with me.

In my ministry, I always have someone to help me check out healings and to help me manage those wanting to testify and those waiting to be prayed for. This one evening, a girl came excitedly to the front. She was thirty-one years old. She pushed through the crowds and came up to me, ignoring my helpers, to tell me that she felt God was going to heal her ear that evening.

I loved her faith, so despite the fact she had somewhat hijacked the meeting, I went with it and agreed to publicly pray with her. It's fair to say she grabbed my hand and placed it on her left ear! I felt a powerful presence of the Holy Spirit.

'What are we praying for, exactly?' I asked.

'I'm deaf in my left ear, and have had lots of preachers pray for me, but I don't know why, I just have faith that it's going to happen tonight. With your hand on my ear, would you just pray? I have faith that God is going to heal me!'

As I finished praying, she stepped back. Slowly, a big smile began to appear on her face as she realised what God had done.

She confirmed that God had carried out His miraculous work and that she could hear. I tested it out, of course. With everyone watching on, we closed the good ear and I whispered into the ear that had not been able to hear. Everything I whispered, she repeated!

Then she got her mobile phone out and started to call someone.

'What are you doing?' I asked, still with everyone watching on and listening in.

'You don't understand!' she said. 'I wasn't just unable to hear. When I was three years old I had cancer of the ear, and my parents had to put me in for surgery. They had to take out my whole inner ear to stop the cancer from getting to my brain. I have nothing to hear with. I literally have a hole in the ear, where the eardrum should be. But I'm hearing! I'm calling my parents!'

The girl went on to explain to everyone that since the age of three, her parents, who were pastors in the United States, had covenanted to pray for her at ten o'clock every night of their lives until she was healed.

'Look at the time!' she said. 'Look at the time!'

It was exactly ten in the evening.

I held the microphone to the mobile. A man answered.

'Dad! It's me.'

'Hi, honey. Is everything OK? It's a strange time for you to call.'

'Dad, you and Mum are praying, aren't you? Right now? For my ear?'

'Yes, honey, we are. It's ten o'clock. That's what we always do. You know that.'

'Dad... Dad... you don't have to. You don't have to pray! God has just healed me. I'm calling now from a meeting in Vancouver. I'm speaking to you using my left ear!'

Suddenly there was a loud cry on the phone. Deep sobbing. Mum shouting for joy in the background. And not a dry face in the meeting either, as we began to appreciate the magnitude of the miracle and the steadfastness of praying parents. For twenty-eight years they had prayed every night. And God had answered. God had answered with a miracle, physically recreating an ear.

Resurrection from the dead

Jesus is in the business of creative miracles, none more so than resurrection from the dead. When someone is dead, there's no use praying for healing. They're dead! If we want to raise the dead, we are talking about a creative miracle. There are a number in the New Testament.

The best example is probably Lazarus. The story is told in the Gospel of John, chapter 11. John tells the story in a clever way. He's been talking about Jesus healing people. And as he launches into this particular chapter, it's as if he is setting us up. He's making us think that there is going to be a healing here too.

After all, this is the family Jesus loved. This is Lazarus. John makes sure we know that Jesus loves this family.[242]

John tells the story: Jesus loves the family, but delays arriving. We expect a healing, as do the family, but Lazarus dies.

And then the amazing miracle. Even though Lazarus has been dead for four days, Jesus raises him from the dead. (Jewish tradition indicates that the spirit of a person leaves their body after three days – so Lazarus is doubly dead!)

There's a shout: 'Lazarus, come forth!'[243] And out of the tomb comes a man who was dead for four days.

Jesus raises the dead. Remember that as His body, we do what Jesus does. Remember the passage that tells us we will 'do even greater things'.[244] Remember that raising people from the dead is specifically instructed by Jesus, directly after the instruction to heal.[245] This is New Testament Christianity!

Witchdoctors and the dead raised

By God's grace, in my ministry so far, I have seen five people raised from the dead. Let me tell you one of those stories.

We were in Uganda and had been having a hard time of things from the local witchdoctor, who had gone onto local radio to condemn the mission we were having, and to curse us. On day three of the mission, the witchdoctor came to the meeting. After a lot of chanting and banging of drums, the man came to the front of the meeting, fell on his face and was saved! Needless to say, faith that God would move was raised further at that point.

It was like an invisible barrier came down and lots of people came to the Lord. It was a fabulous occasion. We had lots of miracles.

One thing was bugging me, though. I couldn't get out of my head the scripture in Acts that says, 'Why should you think it a strange thing that God should raise the dead?'[246] In fact, even before coming out to Uganda, I had felt God prompting me on raising the dead, and to pray for it, with expectation. Every scripture I read seemed to be referring to raising the dead. It bugged me for two months or so before the mission began! At that time, I'd seen a couple of people raised from the dead, but this had been some years earlier. I had stopped telling the stories as they were so far back in time. I felt God was prompting me to tell once more stories of raising the dead, and that He was raising my own faith levels to see this miracle again.

With these promptings from God, with the witchdoctor saved and with the remembrance of the scripture in Acts, I gathered my leaders together at the beginning of the fourth night of the mission. I explained that I felt God was going to do more. That despite the healings so far, we were again going to see miracles – this time someone raised from the dead. I asked them to stand with me for this. They did so in a wonderful way and, with that as background, the fourth night began.

I took a back seat for a lot of the meeting, allowing others to lead. But all the time I was praying to God with an expectation of raising the dead.

Near the end of the meeting, with many testimonies of healing and with a mighty praise time going on, suddenly the crowds parted and I saw four men carrying a body forward. They laid the body on the ground at the foot of the platform we were speaking from. The body of a lady lay there. My brother Paul asked me if I thought the lady was dead. We went down from the platform to see. The body was blue. We couldn't find a pulse.

Spirit of death

When I pray for the dead, I will usually rebuke the spirit of death. Death is a person, a spirit, not just an event. In the book of Revelation, death and Hades are treated as persons, thrown into the lake of fire.[247] So we command that spirit to go. Those of us who believe in Him will not see death.[248] When you come to the end, and you close your eyes, you will see Jesus coming for you, not the spirit of death.

We started to come against the spirit of death and command it to come out, and for life to come into the woman and her spirit to return, in Jesus' name. Within two minutes of starting to pray, the lady suddenly gasped for air, opened her eyes and sat up. Her skin colour returned to normal in front of us. She looked amazed and we asked her what happened.

The lady started touching her stomach, asking the interpreter what had happened to her tumours. I asked what she was saying, and the interpreter explained that she had five tumours around her stomach area and she had come to the meeting believing for a miracle, knowing her diagnosis was not good.

She went on to say: 'I was standing at the back of the meeting and suddenly everything went black. I don't know what happened. I couldn't see anything, and then I saw above me a man dressed in white. I was sure it was Jesus. Then I heard somewhere in the distance, your words. You were saying, "Death, let go of her. Receive life in Jesus' name." And when you said "Receive life in Jesus' name" I saw breath come out of Jesus like a strong wind. It went inside me and I found myself opening my eyes, breathing and looking at you!'

As she was speaking, she was looking down at her body and began to feel her stomach with her hands again.

'They're gone! The tumours have gone! There's nothing there!'

And sure enough, her stomach was smooth. The lumps she described were nowhere to be seen.

Normal New Testament Christianity

What I have just described is normal New Testament Christianity. Too many have come to expect less, but it's all there in the Word. We should expect to pray for the dead to be raised and we should expect resurrection.

If someone has died early – say, before seventy years of age – I believe we should always pray for resurrection. It's not always possible in the UK because of the way the body is kept, and of course, expectations of resurrection are not too high! That's not true of many countries. But wherever we are, I believe the first thing we should do is to gather together around a believer's body and pray for resurrection. Give it a day or so. If we don't get them raised, we release them to the Lord. But we certainly should go for it!

The working of miracles is, of course, not limited to creative physical restorations and the raising of the dead. As we see in Jesus' ministry, walking on water, multiplying food, taking authority over weather patterns and even turning water into wine are all included as 'miracles' He performed. In one sense, even the creation of the heavens and earth are the working of miracles, just on a much larger scale!

I have had several occasions while on the mission field when our financial resources ran out and the money we had literally multiplied in the wallet. When it first happened, my accountant went as white as a sheet, literally shaking as he said to me, 'Something is happening in this wallet, Jon! The money keeps multiplying!' I have sometimes joked that I have tried to get that miracle to keep working ever since… but thank God, when we needed it, heaven's resources were there.

Miracles are God's 'normal'. And they should be our 'normal' too. We have authority over 'snakes and scorpions and … all the power of the enemy'.[249] Demons are subject to us in Jesus' name.[250] We are called to heal the sick and raise the dead.[251] God's kingdom is at hand[252] and we are His ambassadors,[253] His workers, His children. We have the same authority as Jesus and even greater works to do![254]

Do you believe it? Then let's start to live it. Normal New Testament Christianity is faith-filled and action-packed. And why would any of us want to live in any other way than the way God has commissioned us to live?

So don't you see that we don't owe this old do-it-yourself life one red cent. There's nothing in it for us, nothing at all. The best thing to do is give it a decent burial and get on with your new life. God's Spirit beckons. There are things to do and places to go!

This resurrection life you received from God is not a timid, grave-tending life. It's adventurously expectant, greeting God with a childlike 'What's next, Papa?' God's Spirit touches our spirits and confirms who we really are ...[255]

Endnotes

241. Matthew 15:30-31 (NKJV)
242. John 11:5
243. John 11:43 (NKJV)
244. John 14:12 (NIV)
245. Matthew 10:8
246. See Acts 26:8
247. See Revelation 6:8; 20:14
248. Matthew 16:28
249. Luke 10:19 (NIV)
250. Luke 10:17
251. Matthew 10:8
252. Matthew 10:7
253. 2 Corinthians 5:20
254. John 14:12
255. Romans 8:12-17 (The Message)

Chapter Twelve:
The Time is Now!

So, when does this life of kingdom breakthrough, this life of miracles and gospel expansion start? Is it all up to God, or do we have something to do with it? The simple answer is – both. As we have seen, the Holy Spirit is here, and He's ready to convict,[256] convince, heal, deliver and make whole.

What's He waiting for? Us. As simple as that. Jesus said, 'My Father is always working, and so am I.'[257] As we have seen throughout this book, the Holy Spirit is the *parakletos*, the One who comes alongside to help us – not do it for us, but to work through us and with us. So when we move, He moves. Prayer prepares the way and receives the answer in the secret place, but Spirit-led, faith-filled action releases the manifestation of the kingdom in the public place. The time is now!

Faith is now!
The writer to the Hebrews said:

> *Now* faith is the substance of things hoped for, the evidence of things *not* seen.'[258]

Faith deals with the invisible, it speaks and acts on the unseen Word of God and expects God's invisible promises to become manifest realities when we speak and act in line with what God has said. We trust Him with His Word and He trusts us with His power. There's a mutuality in this, a covenant relationship of faith. He is always faithful, and releases revelation and power when we exercise faith in His faithfulness to do what He says.

Such is the nature of the partnership, the relationship the Father has called us into with Himself in bringing about the manifestation of His kingdom rule upon the earth. Faith is '*now*'. It doesn't wait to see everything in the natural world come perfectly into line with God's Word before it acts. True faith is not disturbed by the testimony of the senses. Faith believes and speaks and acts in line with what God says. And God is always speaking in line with what He has spoken. He *is* speaking healing because He *has* spoken healing, He *is* speaking deliverance because He *has* spoken deliverance, He always *is* providing because He always *has* provided.

He is eternally consistent in His nature and will for our lives, and can be trusted to fulfil His promises. My point is, we're on solid ground, so what are we waiting for? Jesus still says, 'Come!' to those who say, 'if it is You…'[259] He will meet us when we act on His Word.

Faith for salvation

In a recent outreach event in Crewe, a heroin addict came into the meeting, together with his friend. They pushed their way past a number of people, upsetting a few as they went, and sat down to listen to what I had to say. Their faces looked like thunder, and they kept murmuring to each other as I spoke. Half way through the message they looked at each other, said something, and got up to leave. I was preaching on the urgency and certainty of salvation, and as they arose, the Spirit of God in me also arose, and I found myself shouting over to them, 'You, sir! Are you certain of heaven? Are you sure where you'd go if you died tonight? Have you received Christ's forgiveness?'

He and his friend stopped in their tracks, looking shocked that I had addressed them directly in the middle of my message.

He said, 'No! I'm not sure...'

'Do you want to be? Will you pray with me now and surrender your life to Jesus Christ?'

'Yes. I want that.'

Moments later he and his friend bowed their heads, closed their eyes, and with tears gave their lives to Christ. That night, the addict was delivered from his drugs, filled with the power of the Holy Spirit, and was out with us on the streets the next day, telling people about the Jesus who saved him and changed him. He brought his girlfriend along the next night who also got saved, and the following Sunday they both got baptised and are now following Jesus in freedom.

I will never forget his parting words to me: 'I am so grateful you made me feel so uncomfortable. If you had not stopped me in my tracks, and spoken to me so directly, I would never have given my life to Christ. But look at me now, my life is changed. Thank you!'

'Now' is the day of salvation. 'Now' is the acceptable time.[260] Don't wait for 'the right time', it may never come. Share Christ today.

Many believers feel the call of God to ministry, to preach the gospel, but are waiting for a pastor to invite them to preach in their church. But the harvest is not in the church, it's in the harvest fields, outside the four walls of our buildings. Don't wait for an invite. Go! It was in the context of the Great Commission, in Matthew's Gospel[261] that Jesus said, 'I am with you always ...' I have never felt His presence more closely with me than since I started to go into all the world, taking Jesus to where the harvest is, to the lost, the hurt and the broken. He is with you. Go in His name, and lives will be transformed by the power of the gospel.

Faith for provision

Some people are called but worry about the money they need to live on or to do various kingdom projects, outreach events and the like. But Jesus sent out the seventy-two with these instructions, 'Carry no money bag, no knapsack, no sandals'[262] and yet later He could ask them, '"When I sent you out .... did you lack anything?" They said, "Nothing."'[263] We must go, trusting God to supply, using what we have first for His kingdom, and then He will supply everything else that is needed:

> [S]eek first the kingdom of God and His righteousness, and all these *things* will be added to you.[264]

When I first started in evangelism, I had no team and no PA system, though I knew I would need one. A pastor in a rural area invited me to come and do a mission for their small local church. He didn't have a PA system either. I had done my homework and worked out exactly the system I needed for that and other missions, and was believing God in prayer for it.

The pastor asked me, just ten days before the mission, 'What should we do about a PA system? Should I rent one?'

I answered him, 'No, don't worry about that. I'll bring mine!'

He thanked me and ended the phone call. I looked up to heaven and said, 'Lord, you heard that!'

Time went by; eight days, in fact. There was no PA system.

I cried out to the Lord, 'I am believing you, Father. I have prayed in faith, and believe I receive what I've asked for, but where is it?'

He answered me, 'You must use what you have first.'

I said, 'Lord, I have no money, what can I use?'

Then He reminded me of £500 that I had set aside in a savings account to do some much-needed decoration in our home. It was all the savings I had.

'Use that,' the Lord said.

I was reminded of the feeding of the 5,000[265] and how often we have to use what we have first and then the Lord multiplies our resources. I stepped out in faith to order the first part of the new system, knowing I needed another £2,000 to complete the order.

To cut a long story short, I am glad to testify that within twenty-four hours of using what I had, of stepping out in faith, the rest of the money came in, mostly from people who knew nothing of my need but felt God prompt them to give me cash or a cheque. I ordered the complete system, which arrived on my doorstep one hour before I was to leave to do that mission. God is faithful!

Sometimes He keeps us believing right up to the last minute, but as so many can testify, He is always on time!

Faith for healing

Many times people are waiting for the leading of the Holy Spirit before they will step out in faith to pray for the sick to be healed. Sometimes He gives us clear direction, and we grow in sensitivity as we spend time with Him in worship, prayer and meditation on the Word of God. But I have found that our hearing and seeing what the Father is saying and doing becomes crystal clear when we become more active in His harvest fields. We don't always need specific direction when Jesus has given us clear instructions to heal the sick. The direction is clear – if they are sick, heal them! And if there are more specific instructions needed in the process of ministering to people, I find He leads us as we go.

While leading a local church in some street evangelism training in the north of England, we went through a period of time where it seemed that nothing much was happening. I paused and looked around to see if the Holy Spirit would draw me to someone in particular, as nobody seemed to be responding to the gospel up to that point. I saw a man in his forties bent over on his crutches, talking to several people outside a pub and, while I had no leading to pray for him, I thought, 'Why not?' I approached him and asked what the crutches were for as he looked like he was in some pain. He told me that two years previously he had fallen down a mountain in the Lake District and broken his hip. He had gone through nine operations without success and to that day the skin surrounding his hip was left open so that surgeons could get to it quickly if it caused him more trouble. He was on high-dosage pain relief, but still spent his days in considerable pain and limited movement. The accident had left one of his legs several inches shorter than the other one.

I asked him if he had any faith in God to heal him. He was quick to respond: 'I'm open to anything.' With the help of a pastor friend of mine, we helped him down onto a seat in the middle of the street, and I went to pray for his leg, so that it would grow out. But the Holy Spirit stopped me and inwardly said to me, 'Tell him to get up and walk!'

I responded, 'Lord, don't You think it would be better for his leg to be lengthened first so that he doesn't trip up when he walks?'

Realising it was not a good idea to tell the Lord how to do His work, I said to the man, 'That's it, get up and walk in Jesus' name!' and then proceeded to lift him up.

The man got to his feet, without his crutches, and started to walk around in utter astonishment as his leg had grown out without us praying for it, and all pain had gone. He kept saying, 'Where's my pain gone, where's my pain gone?' and he walked off down the street with his crutches over his shoulder, rejoicing in God's goodness to him and announcing to us that he was going back to church and recommitting his life to Christ.

Do we always have to have a direct leading of the Holy Spirit to step out in miracles? It's great to have that, and we should always live full of the Spirit and be sensitive to Him, but if we don't have a direct leading, it does not necessarily need to be a limitation, as the Holy Spirit is committed to confirming the Word of God. He moves when we move in faith on the promises of God. Sometimes a sudden rise in faith or sense of determination to see the kingdom come in a situation *is* the leading of the Holy Spirit. Don't be afraid, but only believe.[266] God will meet you there.

The end and the beginning

We have come to the end of this book, but not the end of everything that can be said about partnering with the Holy Spirit. There is always more to say about walking with Him in such a way that He is ungrieved and unquenched[267] … free to do in us and through us everything that reveals Christ authentically to the world. I hope you have enjoyed our journey together. The future is bright with promise, and belongs to those who are willing to leave their comfort zone and step out in faith to embrace the purpose of God.

Make this a beginning. Faith without corresponding action is dead.[268] May I encourage you… the time is *now*… step out and believe God. Greater things await you. The apostle Paul exhorts us that the whole of creation 'waits with eager longing for the revealing of the sons of God'.[269] That's you and me. This is part of the reason for the great emphasis on the Father heart of God in recent years – the Father is revealing the sons. The King is coming, a genuine 'new age' is about to break forth upon the earth. As sons and daughters, we draw our identity from our Father… and if you want to know what He looks like, look at Jesus.[270] This is what the whole creation is longing for – the revealing of the sons. Not the servants, or the ministers, but the sons!

God is calling us back to ministry that flows from relationship, not primarily from a church office or a position in a certain Christian organisation. This is not the possession of a denomination or movement of churches. It's the sons! We all get in on this! Jesus is coming back for a whole bride, not just her eye, ear or foot! God has His ministers who are called to equip the Church, to serve her and bring her to full maturity as a glorious bride. When the Church is fully operating in the grace and power of God, every member ministering, the whole earth will be filled with the experiential knowledge of the glory of God, 'as the waters cover the sea'![271] God has promised it.[272] Let's expect it, rise up and enter into it.

Miracles are just a foretaste of the glory to come. This is your inheritance as a believer in Christ. We get to partner with the Holy Spirit! There is a life of miracles for every believer!

The Greater One who dwells in you wants to be released through you to transform the world. Don't hold back, let Him out; walk and minister with Him and lives will be changed – one life, sometimes many lives, sometimes multitudes at a time. The nations are waiting.

Let's go!

Endnotes

256. John 16:8 (NKJV)
257. John 5:17 (NLT)
258. Hebrews 11:1 (NKJV, author italics)
259. Matthew 14:28-29 (NASB)
260. See 2 Corinthians 6:1-2 (NRSV)
261. Matthew 28:18-20 (NIV)
262. Luke 10:4 (ESV)
263. Luke 22:35 (ESV)
264. Matthew 6:33 (ESV, author italics)
265. Matthew 14:13-21
266. See Mark 5:36
267. Ephesians 4:30; 1 Thessalonians 5:19
268. James 2:26

269. Romans 8:19 (ESV)
270. John 14:10-11
271. Habakkuk 2:14 (ESV)
272. Numbers 14:21

Appendix – Further Study

The following questions and discussion points have been prepared for those of you who would like to study what has been written in more depth. They are useful for personal study, and particularly for home groups and discussion groups.

CHAPTER ONE: THE AUTHORITY OF THE BELIEVER
Questions:

How can we have a power partnership with the Holy Spirit? (Galatians 3:1-5)

Can we expect to do the same miracles that Jesus did? (John 14:12)

Have you been baptised in the Holy Spirit? (Luke 11:9-13)

Discussion:

Where does our authority come from as believers?

Action:

Ask God to fill you/refill you with the Holy Spirit.

CHAPTER TWO: WHAT THE BIBLE SAYS
Questions:

Is 'baptism in the Holy Spirit' a scriptural term? (Acts 1:5; Hebrews 6:1-2)

Compare the 'breathing' of God at the beginning of Genesis with the breath of Christ as described in the Gospels. How does God breathe on us as Christians? (Genesis 2; John 20)

Discussion:

Is the Church called to compassion or to power, or both?

Action:

Reread the Acts of the Apostles. Note the power encounters and how the early believers operated.

CHAPTER THREE: LIVING IT OUT

Questions:

Is it possible to miss out on the baptism of the Holy Spirit? (Acts 19:1-6)

If so, what are the possible consequences?

Discussion:

Read 1 Corinthians 14. How many things are we encouraged to pursue? How do we go about this?

Action:

Ask God to show you what your next steps are in terms of living out the baptism and gifts of the Holy Spirit. Be practical – plan and journal!

CHAPTER FOUR: ENGAGE WITH GOD

Questions:

What are the three categories of the gifts of the Spirit?

How many are open to us to use? (And do we?!)

Discussion:

What balance should we put on looking back at our past life, seeking God for our future ministry, and stepping out in faith 'now'?

Action:

Decide to listen to the Holy Spirit and step out in 'small acts of obedience' this week. Repeat this practice regularly until it becomes a habit in your life.

CHAPTER FIVE: THE PROCLAMATION GIFTS: TONGUES AND INTERPRETATION

Questions:

Can speaking in tongues be for unbelievers as well as benefiting Christians?

Can a Christian speak in more than one tongue? How might this show itself in the believer's life?

Discussion:

Read 1 Corinthians 14:1-4 in different versions/translations. Compare them and discuss how speaking in tongues can help the Christian.

Action:

Set yourself homework each night for a week: before you go to bed, pray in tongues for ten minutes without stopping.

CHAPTER SIX: THE PROCLAMATION GIFTS: PROPHECY

Questions:

Is prophecy always a spoken word? If not, how can it be demonstrated? What is the 'spirit of prophecy'? (Revelation 19:10)

Discussion:

Read 1 John 5:14-15 together and discuss how we can use this scripture confidently in the context of listening to the Holy Spirit.

Action:

Find a quiet place where you won't be disturbed. Speak in tongues for ten minutes or so. Then ask God to speak to you prophetically. Seek a word or picture that will be a blessing to others.

CHAPTER SEVEN: THE REVELATION GIFTS: WISDOM AND KNOWLEDGE

Questions:

Why are the gifts of wisdom and knowledge called 'revelation gifts', and how do they operate?

How can we practically operate in the gifts of wisdom and knowledge?

Discussion:

Discuss how we can know God. What is an 'inner knowing'?

Action:

The Holy Spirit will reveal 'keys' to unlock situations in people's lives when we ask Him. Place a spare key next to your bed. Let it be a visual reminder to you to seek God for words of knowledge and wisdom.

CHAPTER EIGHT: THE REVELATION GIFTS: DISCERNING OF SPIRITS

Questions:

Read 2 Kings 6. How we can look through God's eyes?

In what ways can we guard against the enemy pushing us off track as we seek these gifts?

Discussion:

Grace is not just 'pardon'; it's also 'power'. Discuss how this might be worked out in practice.

Action:

Read the Gospel of Mark. Look for examples of Jesus discerning what was happening in different situations He encountered. Ask God to make you more sensitive to situations you find yourself in, in order to bring God's word of life to people.

CHAPTER NINE: THE POWER GIFTS: GIFT OF FAITH

Questions:

Why is the gift of faith considered to be a 'power gift'?

How does the Word build faith and how does the Spirit encourage us in the Word?

Discussion:

We are encouraged to read, meditate and confess the Word of God in order to move more in the gift of faith. Discuss practical ways we can do this.

Action:

Pray that God will give you an opportunity in the coming week to step out in faith. Prepare yourself in the Word, seek words of knowledge in advance, look for the opportunity and go for it!

CHAPTER TEN: THE POWER GIFTS: GIFTS OF HEALINGS

Questions:

If someone doesn't appear to be healed straight away, what does Scripture say about that? (Consider Romans 8:1; Mark 16:18; Mark 11:24)

Do we have to feel a healing in terms of praying for someone or in receiving healing?

Discussion:

Read Exodus 15:26. Discuss God's promise and how it applies to us as Christians.

Action:

Pray out the promises of healing from Scripture over either a condition you need healing from or one that affects a family member or friend. If for someone else, look for an opportunity to pray with them.

CHAPTER ELEVEN: THE POWER GIFTS: WORKING OF MIRACLES

Questions:

In Matthew 16:28, Jesus says we will not see death. How is this true? How can this 'normal New Testament Christianity' be applied to our daily lives?

Discussion:

Read Matthew 15:30-31 in the NKJV. Consider the difference between the lame and the maimed and discuss how this reflects on the gift of miracles.

Action:

Read John 11 each day for a week and pray for a Holy Spirit anointing on your own life for faith and miracles.

CHAPTER TWELVE: THE TIME IS NOW!

Questions:

John 5:17 says God is always at work. How is He working today? How has this book helped you? What actions are you going to put into place as a result?

Discussion:

Read Hebrews 11:1. Consider how our power partnership with the Holy Spirit is active today. In what ways can we cooperate with the Holy Spirit?

Action:

Faith is for healing, provision and salvation. List ten people you will commit to pray for every week. Begin to pray for them in faith, expect God to work by His Holy Spirit, and look for opportunities to share the gospel with them and lead them to Christ.

More Information

To know more about Jonathan Conrathe's ministry, to book him or members of his team for speaking engagements, missions and conferences, or if you wish to support the ministry prayerfully and/or financially, to receive training for ministry on short term 'impact weeks' or an internship, please contact Mission24:

www.mission24.co.uk
Tel: +44 1778487267

About the Authors

Jonathan Conrathe is founder of Mission24. He has seen in excess of 250,000 people come to a living faith in Jesus Christ over the last thirty years in nearly fifty different nations. He is involved in training evangelists through the Mission24 internship programme, in equipping churches for evangelism and ministry in the power of the Holy Spirit, and he conducts missions in the UK, Europe and further afield. He can also be heard regularly on UCB Christian Radio. Jonathan is happily married to Elaine and they have three boys.

Ralph Turner is team pastor of Mission24. He is an author and blogger. Ralph is married to Roh and they have four adult children and two grandchildren.